Cambridge Elements

Elements in Earth System Governance
edited by
Frank Biermann
Utrecht University
Aarti Gupta
Wageningen University
Michael Mason
London School of Economics and Political Science

LEARNING FOR ENVIRONMENTAL GOVERNANCE

Insights for a More Adaptive Future

Tanya Heikkila
University of Colorado Denver
Andrea K. Gerlak
The University of Arizona

CAMBRIDGE
UNIVERSITY PRESS

Shaftesbury Road, Cambridge CB2 8EA, United Kingdom

One Liberty Plaza, 20th Floor, New York, NY 10006, USA

477 Williamstown Road, Port Melbourne, VIC 3207, Australia

314–321, 3rd Floor, Plot 3, Splendor Forum, Jasola District Centre, New Delhi – 110025, India

103 Penang Road, #05–06/07, Visioncrest Commercial, Singapore 238467

Cambridge University Press is part of Cambridge University Press & Assessment, a department of the University of Cambridge.

We share the University's mission to contribute to society through the pursuit of education, learning and research at the highest international levels of excellence.

www.cambridge.org
Information on this title: www.cambridge.org/9781009461108

DOI: 10.1017/9781009461115

When citing this work, please include a reference to the DOI 10.1017/9781009461115

First published 2024

A catalogue record for this publication is available from the British Library.

ISBN 978-1-009-46110-8 Hardback
ISBN 978-1-009-46112-2 Paperback
ISSN 2631-7818 (online)
ISSN 2631-780X (print)

Learning for Environmental Governance

Insights for a More Adaptive Future

Elements in Earth System Governance

DOI: 10.1017/9781009461115
First published online: April 2024

Tanya Heikkila
University of Colorado Denver

Andrea K. Gerlak
The University of Arizona

Author for correspondence: Tanya Heikkila, tanya.heikkila@ucdenver.edu

Abstract: Learning is critical for our capacity to govern the environment and adapt proactively to complex and emerging environmental issues. Yet, underlying barriers can challenge our capacity for learning in environmental governance. As a result, individuals often fail to adequately understand pressing environmental problems or produce innovative and effective solutions. This Element synthesizes insights from extensive academic and applied research on learning around the world to inform both research and practice. It distills the social and structural features of governance to help researchers and practitioners better understand, diagnose, and support learning and more adaptive responses to environmental problems.

This Element also has a video abstract: www.cambridge.org/EESG_Heikkila

Keywords: learning, adaptive governance, environmental governance, policy learning, environmental change

ISBNs: 9781009461108 (HB), 9781009461122 (PB), 9781009461115 (OC)
ISSNs: 2631-7818 (online), 2631-780X (print)

Contents

1 Introduction

People have been learning about environmental challenges, and how to manage and respond to those challenges, for millennia. The Anasazi people of the southwestern region of what is now North America learned that their communities were not sustainable to persistent and long-term droughts around the thirteenth century, when they abandoned long-term settlements where they had invested in housing, community infrastructure, and agriculture (Benson et al., 2007). Flash forward to the 1800s when people in London began to learn that drinking water was the source of cholera contamination, which led to improvements in how water and wastewater were delivered in modern cities (Johnson, 2006).

By the mid twentieth century, we saw growing evidence of how toxins affect public and environmental health – from the evidence that Rachel Carson brought forth in her book *Silent Spring* and the investigation of the Union Carbide plant disaster in Bhopal, India. By the 1980s, we can observe scientists, advocacy groups, and governments around the world learning about the causes of the destruction of the ozone layer, the importance of ecosystems like equatorial rainforests for carbon sequestration and protection of biodiversity, and the impacts of greenhouse gas emissions on climate change. At the same time, governments and nongovernmental actors have learned diverse ways to address such challenges – from banning highly toxic pollutants, to strengthening the regulation of industrial processes, or creating conservation reserves in forests and oceans – among many other examples of environmental governance.

Environmental governance involves the actions, processes, and products of diverse governmental (e.g., elected officials, regulators, agency staff, governmental researchers, planners) and nongovernmental actors (e.g., private industry, nonprofit advocacy groups, community-based organizations, academics, consultants). Learning can occur at multiple scales of environmental governance (from local to global) and at distinct stages of governance (Gerlak et al., 2018). As actors seek to understand, advocate for, create, implement, and evaluate policies, laws, and programs to manage our planet's air, water, land, species, and other natural systems, learning can play a key role in adaptive and effective governance (Pahl-Wostl et al., 2013; Ison et al., 2015). At the same time, learning by observing environmental governance processes and outcomes can also occur among individuals and organizations outside of formal governance settings.

Despite the evidence of learning in environmental governance, the speed and the depth of learning often do not keep pace with the complexity, dynamics, and uncertainty of environmental systems. Consider the uncertainty underlying just a few of the issues related to the effects of climate change: How do we support healthy ocean food webs with rising ocean temperatures; what types of habitats should governments prioritize for protection as species migrate to more favorable climates; and which communities will be disproportionately harmed by more extreme and more frequent severe weather events? Such questions have global implications and will require fundamental changes to society (Young, 2023) – changes that will need to be driven by environmental governance institutions. Therefore, our governance institutions and the individuals and organizations who shape them, urgently need to learn about the nature, extent, and drivers of new and changing environmental problems and about the strategies and policies that can mitigate or solve them.

The "learning hypothesis" is that new knowledge can foster learning, and that such learning can drive the adaptation of strategies or policies, which in turn can lead to better governance outcomes (Yanguas, 2021). Learning is also seen as a key pathway for influencing the types of collective behavior changes that can support global sustainability (Newell et al., 2022), and as an indicator of the adaptive capacity of environmental governance institutions (Gupta et al., 2010). From a practical perspective, the investments governments make in environmental monitoring, science advisory groups, and program and policy evaluation further suggest that the learning hypothesis is embedded within the design of governance systems.

While the learning hypothesis seems intuitive, in many cases we struggle to learn in environmental governance. Decision-makers often resist or ignore new information and policies are typically slow to adapt, even when we do learn. The result is our collective failure to adequately understand and respond to emerging and highly uncertain environmental issues. We see this with climate change, invasive species, microplastics, increasing use of fossil fuels for blockchain production or artificial intelligence (AI), nutrient pollution in rivers and streams from agriculture, toxins in our building supplies and resultant indoor air pollution, and the list goes on. And worse, some governance processes intentionally prevent us from learning to solve today's most critical problems. For example, through lobbying and misinformation campaigns, the fossil fuel industry has played a key role in blocking efforts to create meaningful policy responses to climate change by the United States (US) federal government over the course of several decades (Oreskes and Conway, 2011; Brulle et al., 2020; Mann, 2021).

One of the explanations for why learning is difficult is that environmental governance systems are complex. Environmental governance systems include:

- national and subnational governments that regulate and monitor environmental conditions;
- regional and international commissions that implement treaties and agreements;

- Indigenous communities who manage lands and resources;
- nonprofits that advocate for the protection of natural resources;
- environmental justice groups who seek protections for communities that are vulnerable to environmental harms;
- industries that pollute the environment and engage in sustainable practices;
- academics who study environmental problems; and
- funders and donors who support environmental research and advocacy, among others.

These actors also engage in an array of formal and informal governance venues and produce decisions across multiple interrelated issues and jurisdictional scales. Yet, it is the very complexity of our governance systems that also makes learning so important.

Despite the challenges, examples of learning to address environmental problems are widespread and growing in the scholarship on environmental governance. Researchers are studying what enables learning and its effects across diverse contexts and locations (Gerlak et al., 2018), including how learning can support change and adaptiveness in governance (Burch et al., 2019; Djalante and Siebenhüner, 2021). Lacking from the literature are lessons on how we can integrate these findings and infuse them into the study and practice of environmental governance to make learning more widespread and intentional. In this Element, we synthesize insights from extensive academic and applied research on learning around the world to inform both research and practice. We distill from this research the social and structural features of governance that can support learning and more adaptive responses to environmental problems.

In doing so, this Element identifies common theoretical foundations of learning in environmental governance, which to-date, have been disjointed across the literature. At the same time, we highlight where literature remains tentative or underdeveloped. This includes offering strategies for how researchers and practitioners can design governance processes and structures to support productive forms of learning. We draw these lessons from extensive empirical research on cases of learning. We recognize that these examples may be biased more toward positive cases of learning (versus cases of non-learning), as well as cases where learning may be more likely – namely more consensual settings (versus conflictual settings). As we discuss more in Section 5, these limitations are also opportunities for pushing learning scholarship forward. Before laying out these lessons in more detail, we take a detour through the Florida Everglades to illustrate how we started learning about learning.

1.1 A Learning Journey in the Florida Everglades

We started our own journey learning about learning over two decades ago as junior professors at Columbia University studying collaborative environmental governance. We travelled to south Florida to interview people working on a joint state and federal program designed to restore some of the natural functions of the historic Everglades. Our interest was in understanding how this program was designed and how it compared with other large-scale ecosystem restoration efforts forming across the US.

Over the course of the mid twentieth century, the Everglades was impaired by urban development, high levels of phosphorous running off from agricultural production, and massive flood control efforts to support such development. The loss of the "river of grass" – or natural wetlands – that once characterized a majority of central and south Florida led to declining habitat for numerous aquatic plants and animals, loss of natural flood mitigation, and destruction of culturally significant landscapes for Indigenous peoples such as the Seminoles.

By the early 2000s, state and federal agencies responsible for managing flood control systems, water supply, water quality, and endangered species in south Florida came together to implement a multibillion-dollar program, called the Comprehensive Everglades Restoration Plan, led by the US Army Corps of Engineers, the leading water management agency in the US. Restoration of the Everglades became one of the largest ecosystem restoration efforts in the world. It involves numerous federal, state, and local agencies, scientists, tribes, and interested stakeholder groups. It has captured the attention of the national media, the National Academy of Sciences, and dozens of scientists and researchers. Although ambitious, the plan raised questions about the feasibility of engineering-based solutions, the benefits of restoration, and how to prioritize actions going forward.

As we metaphorically began to wade into the Everglades, our research uncovered a fundamental question: *Was learning taking place among the various people involved in the collaborative restoration process?* As we dug in, the questions seemed to multiply overnight. How did the individuals and organizations involved collectively understand the complex interactions within the ecosystem? How was the program incorporating ecosystem science and social science into management decisions? What processes existed for participants to learn about the values and preferences of other stakeholders and how could they learn to use that information to prioritize certain restoration actions? How were leaders planning to adapt the management strategies and policies in response to new information and ideas?

We heard these questions repeatedly – from the head of the Everglades National Park in South Florida to Florida's Southwest Water Management District to the head of the US Army Corp's regional office in Jacksonville. New structures and processes were being created to facilitate such learning, including science boards, technical committees, citizen advisory boards, and a task force of diverse stakeholders. Yet, they did not have clear pathways for determining whether or to what extent learning was occurring.

From these observations, we knew we wanted to know more about what makes learning work in these types of governance systems, to better understand what blocks learning, and how people working on complex and uncertain environmental issues can become more adept at learning. These questions led us into the massive body of research around learning among individuals and organizations, and within various policy and governance settings. Using this literature to guide our surveys and interviews with restoration participants in the Everglades, we found many examples of learning. People involved in the Everglades restoration effort identified how they learned about the nature of key challenges, such as water quality issues, as well as how to improve the design and implementation of various restoration projects (Gerlak and Heikkila, 2011).

What was not clear was whether such learning was intentional. It seemed serendipitous. Sometimes a crisis helped spur learning. Other times it was new scientific understanding, such as around phosphorous pollution entering the Everglades from agriculture. Learning happened occasionally when the right people at the right time came together with promising ideas and solid evidence and found some political or organizational will to spur change. At the same time, people involved in the Everglades restoration described examples of blocked learning – such as when new information or science about wildlife habitat was available but the information was not integrated into decision-making about restoration projects. We were, of course, aware that the questions we had about learning were not unique to the Everglades and decided that our own journey into learning should not end there.

1.2 What Is Learning in Environmental Governance

Throughout our journey studying and learning together over the past 20 years, we spent considerable time trying to understand how to measure it and assess it. Likewise, if other researchers, practitioners, or interested stakeholders want to assess the quality and characteristics of learning in places like the Everglades, they too must define it and be able to observe it – an argument we expand upon in Section 2.

1.2.1 Learning as Individuals

To understand learning in environmental governance, we first need a shared understanding of what learning means. As learning involves changes in cognition or behaviors, we usually start with individual-level definitions of learning. You may remember learning how to ride a bike, write a poem, or play the piano as a child. Through those memories, you might see a *process to learning* – such as trial and error, practice, or exposure to new ideas. But learning is not just a process. It is also a *product* or outcome that reflects some change in understanding or beliefs, and/or changes in behaviors or abilities. Figure 1 illustrates these ideas in a highly simplified model. If you could stay on a bike and navigate around obstacles without falling, you could say you learned how to ride a bike.

The fields of developmental psychology, cognitive and behavioral sciences, and education have identified a wide range of individual characteristics that influence how governance actors learn (e.g., see Barrouillet, 2015; Resnick, 2017; Tyng et al., 2017). For instance, individual motivation, cognitive abilities, prior experiences, emotions, attention, and the capacity for self-reflection can play important roles in learning. The ways in which individuals engage in learning processes and the types of learning products that emerge can then reshape or reinforce individual characteristics that support or impede learning. Certain cognitive biases, which we discuss in detail in Section 1.3, can impede learning by limiting what type of information someone is exposed to, or whether they are open to changing their beliefs. As we know from a wealth of political psychology literature, reinforcing existing biases through one's "information bubbles" may create learning feedback loops that focus individuals on only learning from information that supports their existing biases – a phenomenon that fosters political polarization.

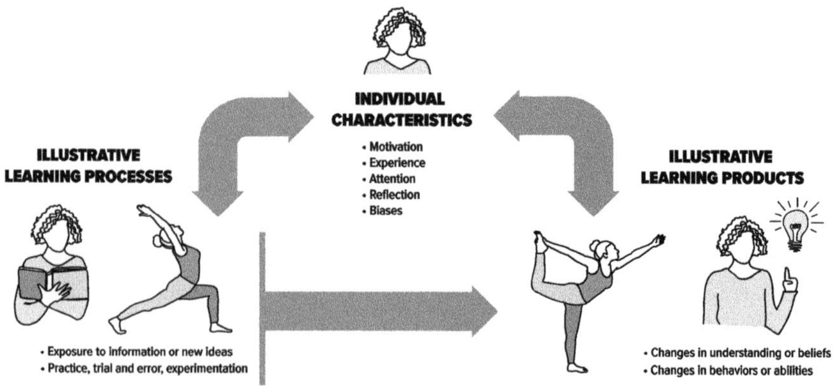

Figure 1 A simplified model of individual learning

1.2.2 Learning Collectively

Learning in environmental governance is not merely about the summation of individual learning in governance processes. Consider a sports analogy. All players on a basketball team can individually learn how to shoot the ball by practicing on their own. The outcome of their learning might be observed by counting their percentage of accurate shots by individual team members. Yet, having a group of good individual players does not mean that the team has learned to play well together. Take the 1969 Los Angeles Lakers, the 1993 Phoenix Suns, or the 2002 Sacramento Kings – professional basketball teams in the US known for having some of the best talent in the league, but they still could not win the national title. To learn collectively, we need the right people and the right processes and structures. A good basketball team, for instance, has players with diverse skills and experience, and usually a talented and motivating coach. The ideas that a coach introduces to the team help foster retention of knowledge and skills, and adaptability of those skills to different contexts. Such learning usually occurs through a well-designed process of practicing together, and a structure that ensures practice will happen at a set time and place. The team can then build strategies, anticipate the approach of the other team, and adapt their strategies when the unexpected happens. Sending each of the players to practice dribbling in isolation will not result in team learning.

Learning together, or collective learning in environmental governance is where groups of people *acquire, translate, and disseminate* innovative ideas about environmental problems or solutions (collective learning "process"), and that process leads to changes in collective understanding or beliefs (collective learning "products") (Heikkila and Gerlak, 2013). As we describe in more detail in Section 2, learning products in environmental governance sometimes focus on technical issues, such as how new chemicals might be contaminating drinking water. Other times, collective learning shifts our understanding of diverse human values toward environmental challenges or of the preferences of different stakeholders for adapting environmental policies (Rodela, 2011; Raymond and Cleary, 2013; Newig et al., 2016). Collective learning products may lead to adaptation or change in governance outcomes. This concept of collective learning is illustrated in Figure 2.

Also shown in Figure 2, governance actors learn within a collective governance "setting" – such as a decision-making venue, an implementation program, or a coalition where actors engage. The collective setting affects both the group, and how individuals within the group learn, along with who teaches. A governance setting that is designed to bring in more diverse forms of knowledge, for instance, could create different incentives for learning than

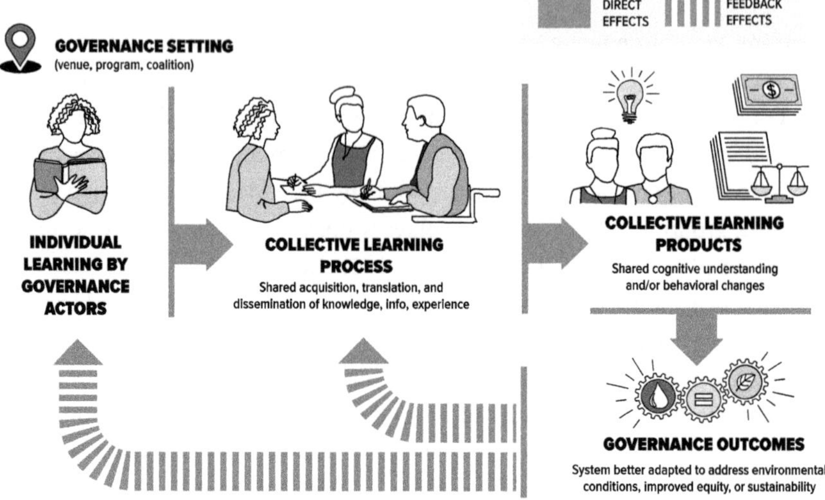

Figure 2 Collective learning in a governance setting

a governance process where knowledge is restricted or controlled by a few actors. Thus, learning is by no means uniform across environmental governance settings, or even across the individual actors within a given setting. Some actors may play more important roles in a learning process, based on their experience, knowledge, networks, or other social factors, which we discuss in Section 3. At the same time, structural features of governance, as we discuss in Section 4 can create differences in who has access to new knowledge, whose information is given more weight or privilege, or whose information can be shared.

1.2.3 Learning Right from Wrong

We do not want to suggest that all learning is productive, or that all learning leads to better environmental governance. History shows us that people learn all kinds of lessons that have negative or unproductive consequences. People can also learn to work only in the interests of those with political power – at the expense of the marginalized. They learn how to resist change or become fragile in the face of new crises or problems. They can learn lessons that reinforce past knowledge and support the status quo. Yet, the lessons we think are good today might look quite different in the future. Indeed, it took decades for decision-makers to learn about the detrimental impact of draining the Everglades. At the time, draining the Everglades was a learned response to flood risk more than a century ago. Similarly, in the Everglades and in many environmental governance processes, it has taken decades to "unlearn" governance practices that exclude environmental and Indigenous values at the expense of agriculture and development interests. Other times, we unlearn lessons too fast, or learning does not stick. After a crisis like an off-shore oil spill, for instance, we might see some immediate lessons about what could have been done differently to prevent the crisis, but that knowledge quickly fades into the background and old patterns persist.

We are admittedly a bit blind to whether or how the insights we offer for infusing learning in environmental governance could foster or reinforce learning the wrong lessons, or whether the learning will stick. Our hope is that we, as scholars, students, and practitioners of governance, can learn about governance processes that teach us bad lessons and correct for these. This assumes that most people are interested in learning beneficial and enduring lessons, especially the people who work diligently toward improving environmental outcomes and sustaining a healthy and livable planet.

1.3 Barriers to Learning

Why is productive learning, or learning the right lessons, so hard when governing the environment? One reason is that environmental governance issues are often complex and uncertain. Too much uncertainty can hinder individual learning or lead to different interpretations of the same evidence (Kahneman and Tversky, 1979). Yet, this complexity and uncertainty is precisely why we need to create intentional learning in our governance processes. The issues we described in the Everglades are illustrative of many of the modern environmental governance issues that policymakers, managers, industry, communities, and advocacy organizations worldwide are struggling to address. More importantly, the interplay among these environmental issues – for instance what hydrological characteristics, temperature levels, and nutrient levels in a water body will trigger a harmful algal bloom event – further hinders our ability to understand them and address them.

Even greater challenges to learning arise when we consider how environmental issues affect different segments of society, especially communities that are vulnerable to environmental harms or injustices. It is not enough to know about who is affected and how if we want to solve these challenges. We also need to learn:

- who has authority and capacity for addressing new or emergent issues,
- how do we garner resources from parties responsible for environmental harms,
- who should have voice and power to represent affected ecosystems and communities,

- what types of environmental governance solutions are preferable for affected or interested communities and stakeholders, and
- how do the benefits and costs of environmental governance choices and actions disproportionately affect vulnerable populations?

When such questions arise in governance processes, they often trigger threats to learning – or an unwillingness to learn about or from those with divergent values and policy beliefs. And in most politicized contexts, such tendencies may lead more to avoidance, or reinforcement of existing ideas, rather than learning new ideas (Heikkila et al., 2020). Even in consensual governance settings, it is rare to find full agreement. Paying attention to the common barriers, such as divergent political beliefs and their potential threats to learning, is a critical and under-studied area of research (Heikkila et al., 2023). As we describe in more detail below, such barriers are often driven by cognitive biases that arise in individual and group decision-making.

1.3.1 Unpacking Cognitive Biases

Cognitive biases can impede learning. One of those biases is that people tend to have negative perceptions toward out-groups and positive feelings for their in-groups (Tajfel and Turner, 1979; Brewer, 1999). In the governance realm where issues are often highly politicized, groups form around shared policy beliefs and political identities, which produce strong in-group affiliations (Mason, 2015). At the same time, people may be unwilling to value information that comes from out-groups with opposing political beliefs or identities. Such "in-group /out-group bias" can also lead people to use only information that aligns with their existing beliefs when making governance choices (Kunda, 1990; Strickland et al., 2011). When people feel their group is threatened by information that counters their beliefs they often react emotionally, which further reinforces their existing positions (Mason, 2015; Mackie and Smith, 2017).

Other cognitive biases in decision-making (Kahneman, 2011) can hinder learning. For example, confirmation bias leads individuals to acquire information that supports their policy beliefs and discount information that does not align with those beliefs (Nickerson, 1998). Likewise, desirability bias drives people to interpret information in support of the beliefs or outcomes they desire to be true (Tappin et al., 2017). Availability bias can also constrain the scope of information or one's ability to learn from it when focusing on information that is closely available or simply top of mind (Tversky and Kahneman, 1973; Sunstein, 2006). Finally, negativity bias can lead people to misinterpret risk, which can block learning (DeCaro et al., 2017) because they overweigh negative information (Baumeister et al., 2001). Each of these cognitive biases, and others, can impede learning in environmental governance by steering people away from relevant information that might help in understanding or addressing pressing environmental issues. Recognizing these barriers and intentionally mitigating their negative effects on learning is necessary for effective environmental governance.

1.3.2 Connecting Individual Barriers to the Governance Setting

Both the cognitive biases that create barriers to learning and the factors that can overcome such biases are shaped by governance settings. For instance, in-group /out-group biases are more likely to be triggered when a governance setting involves low levels of trust or interactions are highly adversarial (Weible et al., 2010; Montpetit and Lachapelle, 2017; Heikkila et al., 2020). Multilevel settings can challenge how and where learning can occur and may create both positive and negative feedback that influence learning (Di Giulio and Vecchi, 2019). As size and diversity of the actors involved increase, governance actors may be exposed to a wider range of views and thus reduce the tendency toward confirmation bias. Yet, in-group/out-group biases can also increase. Likewise, the broader environmental context within which the governance setting is operating might further shape individual biases to learning. Take unexpected environmental crises, like an off-shore oil spill, which can serve as "learning trigger" because it can reveal deficiencies in governance (Deverell, 2009). However, in some cases of extreme surprise and uncertainty, actors may resort to availability bias, status quo bias, or anchoring bias rather than learning (Kamkhaji and Radaelli, 2017). That is, people may retreat to existing beliefs, ignore potentially relevant information, and collective learning becomes blocked – at least within the time that might be necessary to effectively address the problem.

1.4 A Roadmap for Learning in Environmental Governance

Recognizing the challenges to learning (Heikkila and Gerlak, 2013; Gerlak et al., 2018; Heikkila and Gerlak, 2019), researchers, students, and practitioners may wonder *how can people involved in environmental governance learn together intentionally to solve environmental problems?* In examining this question, we draw from more than two decades of our own research on a variety of environmental contexts, and from the rich scholarship and case studies that range from local to regional, to national, and even international scales, produced by many colleagues and peers whose work we closely follow. While our goal is to illustrate and distill lessons from a variety of scales of decision-making and across different countries and political contexts, we are limited by the fact that existing empirical literature draws heavily on local and regional examples from North America, Western Europe, and Australia (Gerlak et al., 2018).

To help situate the empirical evidence, we incorporate insights from a framework we developed from synthesizing diverse bodies of learning scholarship from fields like policy learning, organizational theory and management, adult learning theory, and cognitive psychology (Heikkila and Gerlak, 2013). This framework has been tested in several environmental policy contexts now (e.g., Crow and Albright, 2019; De Voogt and Patterson, 2019; Koebele, 2019; Mukhtarov et al., 2019; Ricco and Schultz, 2019).

In the remaining sections, we move beyond our prior research by reviewing recent studies that align with the insights from our framework. We are grateful for the many theories and frameworks on learning we have been exposed to, the diversity of cases and empirical work from our colleagues over the past two decades, and the many practitioners we have had the privilege to work with and learn from. While the empirical cases and theories found in academic research offer valuable insights on learning in environmental governance, on their own they are incomplete. This Element integrates these insights to offer a holistic, yet practicable, approach to assessing and fostering learning, intentionally, in environmental governance. In doing so, we unpack how the challenges to learning in environmental governance can be overcome with carefully designed social and structural features of governance that infuse learning intentionally into decision-making. As summarized in Figure 3, each of the remaining sections of this Element offer theoretical and empirical lessons for research, teaching, and practice.

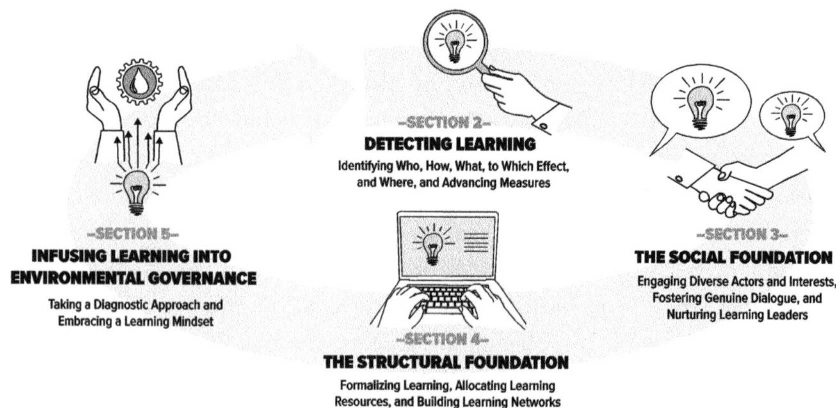

Figure 3 A roadmap for learning in environmental governance

1.4.1 Detecting Learning

In Section 2, we argue that researchers who study environmental governance and the decision-makers involved in designing and implementing environmental governance processes need to pay attention to learning directly and assess it. To help devise a strategy for this, we first distill various theories and scientific studies of learning to identify who learns, how we learn, where we learn, what we learn, and to what effect we learn in environmental governance. We also offer practical examples on how to measure learning in environmental governance.

1.4.2 The Social Foundation for Learning

Section 3 explains how to build the social foundation for learning together in environmental governance. In general, when diverse participants interact regularly to define the problems, share knowledge, and set and implement solutions, learning is more likely. But creating an environment that is conducive to learning is not always easy. Also needed are groups that represent a diverse range of interests, who engage in genuine and face-to-face dialogue, and who have skillful learning leaders acting as brokers between people with competing interests or goals.

1.4.3 Structures to Support Learning

The social elements of governance identified in Section 3 need structures to guide and support learning. Structural features include formal feedback loops to institutionalize learning, dedicated resources to sustain learning, and well-connected venues and organizations that can hard-wire learning across a network.

Sections 3 and 4 discuss several caveats when implementing the social and structural governance foundations we identify. These caveats acknowledge the importance of paying attention to the larger contexts surrounding environmental governance. These contexts include political, socio-economic, and institutional conditions that can influence the feasibility of implementing different social or structural features to support learning into environmental governance.

1.4.4 Infusing Learning into Environmental Governance

Sections 3 and 4 uncover a set of foundational governance features that can guide research and practice, but they are not meant to be a step-by-step recipe. No magic formula exists that works across all organizations or decision-making venues of environmental governance, or that works across all governance questions. Instead, it may be important to infuse learning in a way that allows for continuous adaptation of environmental governance systems and processes.

In doing so, attention should be given to how the social and structural features of governance interrelate and reinforce the capacity for learning. This requires ongoing diagnoses – from academics and practitioners – of how well the individuals and organizations involved in environmental governance are learning and what pieces of the learning puzzle are missing. In the last section of this Element, we encourage environmental governance scholars to infuse learning intentionally into environmental governance by developing a diagnostic approach and building learning systems. In doing so, we offer strategies for how scholars and practitioners can collaborate in advancing intentional learning.

2 Detecting Learning in Environmental Governance

Policy learning. Organizational learning. Social learning. Transformative learning. Collective learning. In the past two decades, a variety of concepts and theories have emerged in diverse bodies of scholarship to characterize learning in governance. What do these various learning concepts mean, and how can we use diverse approaches on learning to improve our capacity to detect and diagnose learning?

The process by which policy actors, or those involved in creating public policy, learn about new policy ideas and translate those ideas into decision-making is a reoccurring theme in policy scholarship (e.g., Heclo, 1974; Howlett and Joshi-Koop, 2011; Dunlop and Radaelli, 2013). Many theories of policy processes employ learning, from the Advocacy Coalition Framework (e.g., Sabatier and Jenkins-Smith, 1999) to theories of institutional change (e.g., Ostrom, 2007), and theories of policy diffusion and policy transfer (e.g., Volden et al., 2008; Butler et al., 2017). Scholars of network governance (e.g., Newig et al., 2010) and collaborative governance (e.g., Gerlak and Heikkila, 2011) similarly see learning as influential in effective and sustainable governance processes. Learning is highlighted in studies of world politics as well, such as in the creation of international organizations (Haas, 2000), or in fostering foreign policy formulation (e.g., Levy, 1994).

Policy scholars are not alone. Researchers of organizational behavior study how individuals come together collectively to learn to improve organizational outcomes (Argyris and Schön, 1997), such as sustainable corporate practices (Zhang and Zhu, 2019). The concept of learning is widespread in nonacademic writings, thought-provoking podcasts, blogs, and magazines. From Peter Senge's (1990) best-selling classic The *Fifth Discipline: The Art and Practice of the Learning Organization* to Amy Edmondson's (2018) *The Fearless Organization: Creating Psychological Safety in the Workplace for Learning,*

Innovation, and Growth, the importance of learning extends well beyond the halls of academia.

The scholarship on environmental governance benefits from and contributes to this rich dialogue around learning. Learning is central to Earth System Governance (ESG) research, especially to the concept of adaptiveness (Burch et al., 2019; Djalante and Siebenhüner, 2021). Learning is a key process for adapting behaviors and policies in response to changing environmental, social, and political circumstances. Although adaptation can occur through other processes – such as political force, mimicry, or manipulation – learning intentionally and reflexively can help ensure that governance choices are better informed and suited to the complex environmental challenges we face. ESG researchers have explored the context, structure, and tools that foster learning (e.g., Rietig, 2021) to improve EGS effectiveness, as well as how issues of agency, scale, and power can promote or block learning (ESG, 2018). Understanding how learning can promote adaptiveness is a key research priority in the next 10 years of ESG scholarship.

Learning is also prominent in theories of adaptive management and adaptive governance (e.g., Walters and Holling, 1990; Pahl-Wostl, 2009). These theories see learning as part of formalized processes that improve management and governance strategies by aligning them with changing information and data. Relatedly, research around disasters and learning (e.g., Crow et al., 2023; Pormon and Lejano, 2023) highlights how people learn to respond and adapt to disasters differently, depending on their institutional and social capacities.

Attention to learning by environmental policy and governance researchers has flourished, yet the field lacks well-defined concepts, shared theoretical principles, and rigorous approaches to measurement (Plummer et al., 2017; Gerlak et al., 2018). This Element can push us toward greater clarity in defining learning and understanding the foundational elements of governance that are associated with learning. At the same time, this Element can offer more sophistication in identifying how social and structural governance elements work together in support of learning, as well as how to assess learning in research and practice more intentionally.

2.1 Key Elements of Learning *Processes* in Environmental Governance

In distilling research on learning, we borrow from Bennett and Howlett's (1992: 275) recommendation to focus on questions such as "who learns, what they learn, and the effects of learning," which other scholars see as useful for studying learning (Moyson et al., 2017; Rietig, 2021). We build from these approaches and show how such questions help flesh out our own definition of collective learning (introduced in Section 1), which differentiates between the process of learning (or "who" and "how") and the cognitive and behavioral products of learning (or "what" and "to what effect"). Finally, we discuss the question of "where" learning occurs, which directs us to consider how the governance setting can be designed to support learning processes and products.

2.1.1 Who Is Learning (and Teaching): Power and Empowerment?

In environmental governance, who learns is a key question. This decision begins with who is invited to the proverbial governance "table," who has power at the table, and who is not at the table. It also begs the question "who is teaching," which influences whose knowledge informs decision-making, along with "what is learned" and "to what effect" as we discuss later. Diverse forms of power can be at play in learning processes, including economic power, informational power, operational power, and social power (e.g., derived from personal skills and knowledge), as well as formal authority and capacity (Roome and Wijen, 2006).

Learning scholars often describe "experts" as both learners and teachers. For instance, policy scholars emphasize the role of policy brokers or policy entrepreneurs to initiate learning processes and facilitate policy change (Howlett et al., 2017; Valin and Huitema, 2023). Similarly epistemic communities, or networks of professionals with expertise, through their knowledge generation and dissemination at both global and local scales in environmental governance, are sources of learning and teaching (e.g., Haas, 1992; Mabon et al., 2019). In addition, coalitions and networks of elite policy actors (e.g., interest groups, industry, environmental nonprofits, universities, and donors), are both teachers (i.e., by sharing their preferences with decision-makers) and learners who can affect policy change (Moyson et al., 2017; Pattison, 2018).

Experts and policy elites are not the only actors who learn (and teach) in environmental governance. The roles of citizens or communities (Pormon and Lejano, 2023) and local or Indigenous knowledge in environmental governance (Bohensky and Maru, 2011) are widely recognized as providing relevant governance knowledge, often grounded in daily experience and practices (Eshuis and Stuiver, 2005). Moreover, by embracing interactions with a broader array of governance actors, the capacity to learn and understand complex issues increases (Pescaroli and Alexander, 2018). In other words, who learns, and who teaches, in environmental governance should be examined from a broad lens that acknowledges the roles of diverse types of actors, particularly those who traditionally do not have power in government.

One of the ways local and Indigenous actors might have opportunities to both learn and teach in environmental governance is through collaborative knowledge production, or co-production processes (e.g., Baker et al., 2020; Turnhout et al., 2020). In these processes, knowledge users and producers interact to develop tailored information fit for purpose. The extent of that learning, and whether certain individuals play more central roles in collective learning (e.g., leaders, knowledge brokers) relative to traditionally marginalized groups, however, can depend on various governance characteristics, such as the quality of interactions between groups (Baker et al., 2020; Norström et al., 2020) – which we describe in more detail in Section 3. It may also depend on how much agency marginalized groups are afforded to self-define their roles, responsibilities, objectives, and priorities (Turnhout et al., 2020) – a consideration for learning structures we touch upon in Section 4. Ideally, learning processes under any approach would empower community members in ways that help build broader resilience and sustainability (Pormon and Lejano, 2023).

2.1.2 How We Learn Together: Acquiring, Translating, and Disseminating

Collective learning unfolds through a process of acquisition, translation, and dissemination of knowledge, information, and experience (Gerlak and Heikkila, 2011). The acquisition phase involves the collection or receipt of information. Information can be acquired experientially, through searching and noticing, practice and conditioning, and through trial and error (Fazey et al., 2005). Organizations may also engage in self-appraisals, experiments, or assessments (Schneider and Ingram, 1990; Walters and Holling, 1990) to gain information that can allow actors to learn about errors or problems or how processes have been unfolding over time.

Through translation, which involves interpreting the meaning of new information, information is understood and becomes shared knowledge. Individuals, groups, and networks may seek out sources of expert knowledge or rely on trusted advisors to help interpret information (Heikkila and Gerlak, 2013: 489). Subconsciously, mental framing, individual habits, professional training, and behavioral patterns may create "ways of knowing" that influence translation of ideas across diverse members of a group (Lejano and Ingram, 2009).

Finally, individual-level knowledge within a collective group develops into shared knowledge through dissemination, or the transference and embedding of information across a group (Argote, 2011). Dissemination can occur in a variety of ways, such as through collective routines and shared communication processes (Feldman and Rafaeli, 2002). Storytelling can also help promote dissemination because it can help individuals within a group relate to new information about problems or new approaches or solutions (Crossan et al., 1999).

The phases of collective learning are not always differentiated or directly observed when studying learning in environmental governance. For instance, researchers of social learning focus on interactions between people as the primary way individuals learn (Armitage et al., 2008; Pahl-Wostl, 2009). Lejano and colleagues (2021) emphasize the process of mutual development and sharing of knowledge through iterative reflection on observation and experience.

Others pay attention to specific mechanisms that feed into multiple stages of learning. By "mechanism" we are referring to a pathway that brings an outcome, such as learning, into being, or a process that triggers the multiple stages of learning. For instance, storytelling can be a powerful process not only for disseminating information, but also helping people acquire knowledge about marginalized groups (Adelle et al., 2022), interpret information more intuitively (Goldstein et al., 2015; Boris, 2017), or make sense of nonroutine, uncertain, or novel situations (Bietti et al., 2019). Similarly, scenarios are commonly used to help people acquire information about possible alternative futures, and then interpret how that information connects to present actions and decision-making around risk and uncertainty (e.g., Marchau et al., 2019; Gerlak et al., 2021a).

2.2 Key Elements of Learning *Products* in Environmental Governance

2.2.1 The "What" in Learning: Not All Learning Is the Same

Learning researchers commonly discuss *what* individuals, groups, and organizations learn in governance processes, often as "types" of learning. May's (1992) classic typology (e.g., see Bennett, 1997; Meseguer, 2005) includes: political learning, which is learning about the strategies or tools to influence policy; instrumental learning, or learning about the feasibility and effectiveness of policy implementation; and social policy learning, which is about the definition or social construction of a policy issue. Other typologies refer to conceptual versus technical (Nilsson, 2006) or more cognitive versus relational kinds of learning (Armitage et al., 2018; Huitema et al., 2010). Others differentiate between non-learning, where no information is processed, and blocked learning, where learning occurs but is not translated or disseminated into group knowledge or action (Vagionaki, 2018).

Some typologies of learning blend how learning occurs with what types of learning arise. Rietig (2019), for example, suggests three basic archetypes of learning: factual learning, experiential learning, and constructivist learning. While factual learning focuses on *what* knowledge is gained, experiential learning is about *how* engagement in a governance process produces a different type of learning. Likewise, constructivist learning is about *what* changes to beliefs result from processes that are "more than a reflection on the input and a resulting increase in knowledge or experience" (Rietig, 2021: 165). This concept of constructivist learning is like reflexive learning (e.g., see Dunlop and Radaelli, 2013), which is about a reflexive mode – or *how* learning occurs – and resulting changes in preferences – or *what* learning occurs.

In our own work, we categorize what is learned into both cognitive and behavioral forms of learning (Heikkila and Gerlak, 2013). Cognitive learning is about what changes occur in the minds of individuals. They can include changes in factual understanding, knowledge of political strategies or even changes to core values and beliefs. The behavioral manifestations of learning involve changes to strategies, rules, or policies in response to new information.

These diverse typologies of what is learned, and their intersection with how learning occurs, have led to messiness in research design and conceptualization. Still, typologies of learning can be useful for developing more nuanced theories and hypotheses of how or why different types of learning may emerge. They also can allow researchers to develop insightful comparisons of learning products across governance settings and contexts. Doing so might then enable us to trace whether who learns, where governance actors learn, and how they learn can shape what they learn.

2.2.2 "To Which Effect": Depth and Breadth of Learning

What is learned, and often how learning happens, are often characterized – whether explicitly or implicitly – in terms of their depth. The concept of "loop" learning is perhaps the most common categorization of learning depth. Single-loop learning involves the detection and correction of errors, which allow organizations to implement their objectives and norms, while double-loop learning goes deeper by modifying those norms and objectives (Argyris and Schön, 1996). Certain learning processes, such as knowledge co-production, are more often linked to double-loop learning because they enable governance actors to gain insights into varying perspectives and understandings of policy solutions. Triple-loop learning goes even deeper by examining how we learn about and eventually change underlying governance norms (Johannessen et al., 2019). Researchers studying adaptive environmental governance often see triple-loop learning as key to improving governance processes and building capacity to better respond to uncertain environmental changes (Armitage et al., 2008).

From an individual learning perspective, deep forms of learning occur when people overcome prior experience – or experience that could result in inappropriate choices when facing complex or dynamic situations – and adapt their decisions to information about new circumstances (Ohlsson, 2011). Deeper forms of learning can eventually transform groups and social processes (Mezirow, 1994). Such "transformative learning" in environmental governance allows participants to construct new cause–effect relationships, which can lead to more integrated, sustainable solutions to difficult environmental problems (Sims and Sinclair, 2008). Others describe these deeper forms where participants change preferences of learning as "thick" learning, as opposed to "thin" learning, where participants simply learn to cope with a problem without changing preferences (Radaelli, 2008: 244). Similarly, deliberative learning (Dunlop and Radaelli, 2013) where actors co-create knowledge and governance solutions, can lead to new ways of knowing (Lejano and Ingram, 2009) that would not be feasible without deliberation and reflection.

In addition to the depth of learning, the breadth of learning can be an important consideration in environmental governance. The breadth of learning raises questions such as how many actors involved in governance are learning together, to what extent learning is shared across individuals or organizations in a network, or to what extent the coordination of actors in a polycentric governance system allows for learning across venues (Bodin, 2017). Although the scholarship on learning in environmental governance tends to focus on exploring the depth of learning, potentially important considerations about the quality of learning, such as how power struggles play out in learning processes (e.g., Betsill and Bulkeley, 2004), can be assessed when accounting for questions around breadth. Empirical studies in fact suggest that learning among only a few key policy actors may be necessary to effectively push lessons into policy action (Rietig and Perkins, 2018). Thus, considering the breadth of learning, when examining "who" learns, can open important theoretical and practical questions.

2.2.3 "Where" Learning Happens: Diverse Governance Settings

Learning in environmental governance takes place within a wide variety of institutional locations and places, decision processes, or forums and venues (Gerlak et al., 2018), which we described in Section 1 as the governance setting. Sometimes these settings are more formal and institutionalized like a regulatory venue or a commission for an international environmental treaty. They can also be informal and ad hoc such as a group of citizen scientists who share data on air quality monitoring with a government agency or nonprofit group, or a task force of people brought together to provide advice on an emerging environmental issue. Alternatively, learning might occur within subgroups of venues, such as a leadership committee, or across a network of local government leaders working on climate change. Whether formal or informal, governance settings can range in jurisdictional scale – from local to regional, national, and international – and in size, geographic scope, and institutional complexity.

The characteristics of governance settings where learning can occur are important because they establish both the social foundation (see Section 3) and the structure (see Section 4) that shape collective learning. For instance, the structure dictates who learns or who is empowered to learn, and what types of social interactions or processes of learning are supported and allowed. As Dunlop and Radaelli (2013) recognize, different modes of learning are triggered by institutional contexts, such as hierarchies versus epistemic communities. Some settings might have design features that intentionally enable learning – such as policy labs that engage in experiments. Venues also can create different barriers to learning or exacerbate individual learning barriers (Heikkila et al., 2023). In their study of large, diverse forums for national-level climate deliberation, Wagner and Ylä-Antilla (2020) find that actors opt to interact with those already in their network who share their beliefs. In doing so, climate policy actors narrow the scope of learning.

Likewise, when trying to observe and diagnose *where* learning occurs in environmental governance, the complexity of the governance structure can be important to consider. For instance, in highly polycentric governance systems with multiple overlapping venues, the structure of these systems can have critical implications for *how* learning occurs. Moreover, as the boundaries or scope of the governance system become more complex, certain characteristics of the system, such as its connectivity, may become more important for learning.

2.3 Advancing Measures of Learning

Researchers of learning have adopted a diverse set of approaches to detect and measure learning in environmental governance. Document analysis, interviews, and surveys are common tools (Crow and Albright, 2019; De Voogt and Patterson, 2019; Koebele, 2019), Others use process tracing and ethnographic approaches (Mukhtarov et al., 2019), participant observation (Rietig, 2019; Ricco and Schultz, 2019), or cognitive mapping (Huitema et al., 2010). How scholars measure and study learning depend upon whether they are interested in a particular piece of a learning process or a learning product and which level of analysis within a governance context (e.g., individual actors, policy venues, collaborative groups, or networks) is most relevant for their learning questions at hand.

Researchers have struggled with measurement and operationalization challenges, especially around the connection between learning processes and products, and between learning and environmental governance outcomes (Siebenhüner et al., 2016; Armitage et al., 2018). Part of this challenge is due to the latent nature of learning – and our inability to see it directly. We often use proxy indicators, such as changes in behaviors or actions that might arise through processes other than learning (like force). Other times we use self-reported perceptions of learning, which can be biased by social desirability to report learning. Additionally assessing collective learning using measures based on the responses of individuals remains a perennial challenge (e.g., see Montpetit and LaChapelle, 2015). For instance, how many individuals must learn to say that the collective has learned? In addition, learning as a process can easily be conflated with changes in policies or outcomes (Muro and Jeffrey, 2012). Challenges also arise around the temporal dimension of learning. Learning sometimes takes more time than researchers have available to study learning. So, we might be able to detect learning processes, but fail at detecting the products or outcomes.

Despite these limitations, we have observed significant improvement in the measurement and conceptualization of learning in recent years. We see more attention to explicit conceptual definitions and operationalization, more sophisticated measurement approaches using multiple methods, and more rigorous analytical tools – both using qualitative and quantitative methods – and advancements in observing learning over multiple time periods. Gronow and colleagues (2021), for example, measure learning in policy networks that are involved in reducing emissions from deforestation. They provide direct evidence of how belief change, as a form of learning, happens and how different network structures shape learning. Others have used experiments (e.g., Yu et al., 2016) to measure learning processes, and outcomes. We have also seen signs of more engaged scholarship approaches. Ricco and Schultz's (2019) study, for example, engaged with US Forest Service employees during discussions of forest plan revisions, with follow-up interviews, to inform their study of learning.

Developing clear measures and approaches for assessing learning processes and products is not simply an academic exercise. From a practical perspective, the who, how, what and to which effect of learning gives us some diagnostic tools that we discuss further in Section 5 for assessing learning in practice. Identifying different types of learning might be useful for thinking more critically about what type of learning may be needed to solve shared problems. Focusing on instrumental learning or more technical forms of learning, for instance, may not improve governance outcomes when the underlying source of an environmental problems is that people simply hold different values about the importance or relevance of the technical issues.

Disentangling the characteristics of the governance setting (*where*) from the process (*who* and *how*) and products (*what* and *to which effect*) further is important for identifying and testing the learning hypothesis. The hypothesis assumes that the environmental governance setting (*where*) can influence *how* learning happens and *what* results from it. It also helps separate some of the bundled concepts in learning – like relational learning, which assumes both a process of dialogue and a learning outcome of improved understanding of relations. By unpacking these elements, we might discover that a governance process emphasizing dialogue and communication among diverse stakeholders triggers an unwillingness or inability to learn about one other's values, rather than triggering relational learning. What might matter in such a process is not just that diverse stakeholders are present, but whether the dialogue is facilitated and what resources are in place to support engagement. We draw out what types of social and structural foundations of environmental governance are more likely to support learning in the next two sections.

3 The Social Foundation for Learning

More than a decade ago, in Tucson, Arizona, US, city leaders started working together to expand green infrastructure through water harvesting programs (Gerlak et al., 2021b). The engineering and planning tools to build green infrastructure for multiple benefits, including flooding risk reduction, heat island mitigation, reduced energy consumption, and enhanced air and water quality, were well-known. The challenge was figuring out how to ensure that the access to green infrastructure, and its benefits, would be equitable for the diverse communities that live, work, and recreate in the city. Fundamentally, this meant learning how people in Tucson would use green infrastructure, where they wanted it located, and how to balance those needs with other community values like education, recreation, or wildlife protection.

Getting the right people involved to talk about green infrastructure was not easy. City of Tucson officials charged with developing this infrastructure faced hurdles when trying to coordinate with other city departments with distinct cultures and mandates. And officials did not always have the right approaches to identify community partners and local citizens. But they recognized the importance of getting key stakeholders together. "We don't often know what we don't know," shared Blue Baldwin, Program Manager for the city's new Storm to Shade Program."[1] We need to engage with diverse people in our city to truly be able to understand the landscape around green infrastructure and craft meaningful solutions to the challenges we face." For Xochitl Coronado-Vargas Public Outreach Coordinator for the program, "it is about understanding the diversity of people, perspectives, and cultures in our community. Engaging with

[1] Personal communication, November 18, 2022.

narrow, homogenous groups of people limits our understanding. We need to engage, educate, and learn from others."[2]

Learning how to develop green infrastructure in Tucson came down to getting relevant stakeholders to the table and facilitating productive stakeholder interactions. As with most environmental governance processes, the people involved and their interactions determine what information will be shared, how they interpret that information, and how they disseminate it (Carlile, 2004). In other words, the social features of environmental governance are critical to learning (Heikkila and Gerlak, 2013).

In this section, we draw from extensive research to identify three main features that comprise the social foundations for learning: (1) engaging diverse actors and interests, (2) fostering genuine dialogue, and (3) nurturing skilled learning leaders. Each of these features can be activated through multiple mechanisms, which we illustrate below. Mechanisms in social science are often critical for understanding complex causal pathways and the processes by which an outcome emerges. As we alluded to in Section 2, a variety of mechanisms can trigger learning. The mechanisms we identify may not represent all the ways to activate the social foundations for learning. They offer a starting point for researchers interested in developing learning theory, while also helping practitioners identify strategic steps to establish these social foundations in governance processes. They also do not necessarily operate independently. While we discuss them individually, we recognize that they may reinforce one another.

3.1 Engaging Diverse Actors and Interests

Engaging diverse people in environmental governance offers new sources of knowledge and opportunities for learning. For instance, green infrastructure leaders in Tucson intentionally engaged with disenfranchised communities through new low-income rainwater harvesting programs and by building community relations. They did this project-by-project, and in cooperation with other city initiatives. Drawing together individuals and organizations whose interests and values around a governance issue differ, especially people who historically were excluded from governance processes, can stimulate openness to novel ideas (Siebenhüner, 2008). Empowering marginalized groups also mitigates past power imbalances in environmental governance that constrain learning around narrow perspectives, enhancing capacity to solve complex problems (Bendt et al., 2013). Bringing together a diversity of interests is not as simple as it sounds. It requires bringing the right mix of people together for the problem and going beyond the usual suspects.

[2] Personal communication, November 18, 2022.

3.1.1 Find the Right Mix of People for the Problem

Environmental problems are complex. Learning to address this complexity requires insights from people who bring different perspectives to bear on these problems. Not everyone affected by an environmental governance action, decision, or program, knows in advance that they need to be at the table. Furthermore, the definition of stakeholders or community is often unclear in environmental governance processes. Yet, how we define stakeholders or community determines who gets to be engaged (Bendtsen et al., 2021), and therefore who learns and who governance actors learn from.

Over a decade ago, the threat of high valued fish species collapsing in the United Kingdom (UK) triggered a process where diverse stakeholders engaged in dialogue and learning. The threat of the banning the sale of skates and rays "caused shock waves throughout the fish supply chain," according to researchers at England's University of Hull (Garrett et al., 2012: 184). A series of workshops brought together retail companies, scientists, managers, and working fishers to better understand the scope of the problem and develop potential solutions. The outcomes of these processes included an enhanced understanding of the different situations facing these species, a database to provide timely trade information, and an identification guide to assist fishers. Around the same time, the UK government was threatening to prevent access to parts of the most productive UK scallop fishing grounds through the designation of marine protected areas. Voluntary closed areas were introduced in a few bays across Scotland, Wales, and England but breaches in the agreements resulted in statutory closures in a few bays. Fearful of these closures, the scallop industry brought together a diverse group of stakeholders to counter the negative publicity surrounding the industry and to "moderate proposals to prevent access to scallop grounds" (Garrett et al., 2012: 185). Stakeholders included conservation agencies, voluntary wildlife trusts, processors, retailers, and scallop fishers. These stakeholders devised a plan to pilot new fishing gear aimed at reducing habitat damage, improving catch quality, and cutting fuel consumption.

In both cases, the diversity of actors across industry, government, nongovernmental organizations (NGOs), and scientists brought essential, but distinct perspectives on the problem of overfishing. The conversations were not limited to fisheries scientists and policymakers. By engaging more diverse actors and interests, the process allowed for learning about the science-informed tools that industry could use in collaboration with policymakers to create more feasible solutions.

3.1.2 Go Beyond the Usual Suspects

When diverse types of actors are at the table, sometimes those actors are the usual suspects. The usual suspects are often the people and organizations who regularly voice their positions on environmental governance issues, or who are well-known in a specific governance community. A typical regulatory hearing on an environmental issue for instance might include environmental nonprofits, regulated industry, advocacy organizations, and other related government agencies. Although diverse in terms of the organizations they represent, such a mix of actors may lack creative insights or lessons from outside their system that can foster learning and innovation in governance. Going beyond the usual suspects might involve bringing in more local communities when developing projects or environmental solutions targeted at local issues and problems (Folke et al., 2005). Similarly, Indigenous knowledge, or traditional ecological knowledge (TEK), brings essential historical understanding of environmental issues and experience on how to manage natural resources (Bohensky and Maru, 2011).

Since western science is often privileged in environmental governance over other forms of knowledge, creative approaches that start early in decision-making processes often are necessary to incorporate alternative types of knowledge. The Glen Canyon Adaptive Management Program in the US follows a mix of strategies to access diverse forms of knowledge (Gerlak et al., 2021c). Created in 1992, this federal program coordinates dam operations, downstream resource protection, and monitoring in the Glen Canyon region of the Colorado River. In this program, stakeholders can raise emerging issues and invite experts in to present to the larger group, allowing for an influx of outside ideas. Efforts have not always been ideal, however. In response to growing tribal dissatisfaction with the Glen Canyon process, in 2012, the Cultural Resources Ad Hoc Group proposed the inclusion of TEK as a pilot project. The group suggested that the culture of science failed to represent humanistic values and acknowledge a role for Indigenous communities in the program. To rectify this, in 2015 the first-ever Tribal Consultation Plan outlined a process to seek, discuss, and consider the views of Tribes and exchange ideas, not simply providing information.

Another example of creative approaches for bringing diverse stakeholders into the mix is highlighted in an urban forestry program in Melbourne, Australia (Gulsrud et al., 2018). The city developed several in-person and online forums to intentionally create opportunities for learning around urban forestry. Through their efforts, they brought in voices less frequently heard in community engagement forums. For example, they hosted local in-person forums in neighborhoods across the city at various times of the day and week. They engaged youth in envisioning their local urban landscapes through an art competition. They designed review councils composed of demographically representative citizens to engage in discussions around urban renaturing. Finally, the city created an online platform where citizens can learn about specific trees across the city, which included individual email address for each tree species so citizens could send their thoughts and feelings, or questions about specific trees.

Through these approaches, citizens learned about how proposed strategies could accommodate citizen goals for the neighborhood. They also learned how these goals would fit alongside the city's indicators of urban forest health like aesthetic preferences and tree planting and removal strategies. Adding to the fun, children actively contributed by drawing neighborhood maps with their favorite trees and plants. In the end, Melbourne's citizens helped establish 10 urban forest precinct plans through a process involving a more diverse set of people than the city had in past processes. Based on citizen input, the city implemented a long-term strategy to invest in urban green infrastructure with the aim of promoting landscape resilience and community wellbeing. Ironically, when they first initiated the process, City of Melbourne officials had thought the effort would lead to a tree removal as a drought response strategy in the face of climate change. However, the lessons learned through the various community engagement activities were more transformative than what the city had imagined – leading to novel management actions.

3.1.3 Watch Out for Pitfalls When Engaging Diverse Interests

Not all processes that include diverse actors and interests will foster learning. Power differentials or priorities of dominant actors can be challenging. In a study of municipal flood risk governance in the Netherlands, local priorities and understandings of risk directly affected the degree to which municipalities were likely to use information provided by external sources (De Voogt and Patterson, 2019). Similarly, researchers studying municipal climate change governance in Durban, South Africa found that strong personalities served as gatekeepers and barriers to external expertise, as experts were perceived as being out of touch with local realities (Leck and Roberts, 2015). As a result, department officials narrowly focused on developing and strengthening internal knowledge sources. Sometimes social features reinforce in-group/out-group biases. Participants may gravitate toward those who are most like them, which can reinforce negativity biases toward dissimilar groups (Brewer, 1999). Engagement approaches that encourage diverse participants to see themselves as the "other," and not as the center of expertise can help overcome these challenges (Palmer, 2011).

A fundamental challenge of bringing together diverse people is that they may not speak the same language, including technical languages often adopted in governance processes. They also may not be capable of translating ideas into lessons that are directly applicable to the context of the governance system. It can take considerable time to build a shared or common language to help translate ideas in similar ways and come to agreement on these ideas (Richerson and Boyd, 2005). But, when diverse groups of people build a common language, they engage in deeper forms of learning and become more capable of accurately understanding those individuals or groups with competing interests and beliefs. They also are more likely to overcome some of the individual cognitive biases that can impede collective learning. In the case of Melbourne, Australia's urban forestry efforts, city officials came to see how their intentional efforts to promote learning helped to develop a common language for the community and even served to promote deep learning and transformation among the most vocal and skeptical citizen groups (Gulsrud et al., 2018).

Despite some of the difficulties that can arise in more inclusive processes, the benefits of bringing diverse interests together likely outweigh the alternative. Limiting participants to a narrow band of interests can lead to poorly informed decisions. Take an example from community wildfire protection planning in the eastern US. Researchers from the University of Minnesota and the US Forest Service found that when participation is limited to certain individuals – in this case, state and local foresters and fire chiefs – a narrow type of institutionalized knowledge of wildfires was present (Brummel et al., 2010). Because the groups primarily consisted of traditional agency partners, they focused on existing management goals of fire suppression and fuels mitigation. This resulted in a less innovative approach to designing new practices and constrained learning.

3.2 Fostering Genuine Dialogue

For learning to occur among diverse governance actors, *how* they engage may, in fact, be even more important than *who* engages (Newig et al., 2019). When bringing diverse interests together, well-designed, genuine dialogue can help people access and disseminate information necessary for learning (Lipshitz et al., 2002), while also building novel ways of understanding environmental issues (Lejano and Ingram, 2009). Genuine dialogue, however, requires fairness – ensuring equal time and opportunity for everyone to express their ideas and to listen to each other. In the Tucson green infrastructure example, various stakeholders came together in 2021 specifically to develop a participatory, community-based approach to maintaining green infrastructure in the city. Through a series of workshops, as part of a larger university-community partnership, various stakeholders shared their perspectives and expertise related to funding, practicalities of maintenance, and technicalities of soil and plants (Gerlak et al., 2022). In subsequent efforts, engagement specialists working for the city on green infrastructure shifted to interactive, open house formats. These formats provide participants with access to diverse stakeholders in informal settings. Again, genuine dialogue does not simply happen when you invite people to engage. Several key conditions are necessary, which include building mutual respect, using creative approaches, and sustaining dialogue.

3.2.1 Create Mutual Respect Through Face-to-Face Interaction

Face-to-face interaction, built on respect and equity, is a key feature of genuine dialogue (Pahl-Wostl et al., 2007a; Gerlak et al., 2018). Respectful, face-to-face interactions where mutual criticism is tolerated can support learning and greater group creativity (Ohlsson, 2011). This can be particularly important where people have different mental frames or ways of knowing based on their experience or connection to an environmental issue. Diverse perspectives and opinions, expressed in a mutually respectful manner, can allow people to question their own assumptions and envision new or different futures (Innes and Booher, 1999).

Ensuring a climate of respect is especially important for vulnerable or disenfranchised groups. When Thai farmers were treated respectfully by public irrigation staff in participatory irrigation management meetings, they were more open to diverse points of views and willing to learn different perspectives from fellow farmers (Kumnerdpet, 2011). At the same time disrupting unequal power relationships and investing in trust-building are often essential to fostering learning (Davidson-Hunt and O'Flaherty, 2007).

3.2.2 Use Creative Approaches

Opportunities for dialogue that involve more creative, and playful approaches, such as simulation gaming approaches (Haug et al., 2011), scenario building (Innes and Booher, 1999), field trips (Gerlak and Heikkila, 2011), brainstorming, participatory modeling, and cognitive mapping can support learning. Researchers studying adult learning in activist organizations similarly find that using humor and other creative approaches, such as reading circles or knitting groups, can spur learning about activist goals and strategies (Ollis, 2020). Through such approaches, governance actors can examine their beliefs in relation to others and learn about the dynamics of social-ecological systems (Özesmi and Özesmi, 2003). Such approaches also allow for informal discussion and developing trust (Sinclair et al., 2011), which can support learning.

One example is "mental modeling," which elicits people's internal beliefs about an external reality – such as environmental conditions – and makes those models explicit. Mental modeling exercises, through a series of participatory workshops, helped community members learn about and devise natural disaster strategies in Hawaii's North Shore of Oahu (Henly-Shepard et al., 2015). The mental model exercises drew out community members' beliefs about the natural hazards they were facing, and their perceptions of trade-offs in different adaptation responses. These activities allowed participants to first learn about each other's understanding of the community system, build trust and empower participants. They also developed strategies to reduce hazard risks to the community. Researchers documented changes in participants' mental models of natural disasters, finding that people progressed from more superficial to deeper forms of learning over the course of the workshops.

"Serious games" can also provide interactive ways to engage diverse participants in environmental governance. Serious games are useful learning processes when incomplete knowledge, diverse cultural norms, or concerns with power asymmetries exist (Rodela et al., 2019). In the Cedar River Watershed in eastern Iowa, disciplinary experts, policymakers, and local stakeholders played the multi-hazard tournament, developed by Agriculture and Agri-food Canada (Hill et al., 2014). It educated and trained participants in decision-making skills around drought and water (Bathke et al., 2019). Participants were organized into teams and charged with crafting solutions for reducing flood, drought, and water quality impacts under climate scenarios. In addition to the game players, they had referees dressed in costume, team facilitators, fans, and an announcer. The game format consisted of (1) a scenario presentation, (2) facilitated discussion of the scenarios, (3) adaptation option selection, (4) crafting of a press release, and (5) scoring. Each of the seven teams had a $1.6 billion budget in the first scenario for adopting water management strategies for a 20-year planning period. Subsequent rounds decreased budgets and incorporated maintenance and operating costs and introduced hazards like flood and drought. Players engaged with new individuals across sectors and worked collaboratively through the scenarios. They gained knowledge about water management options and strengthened their ability to evaluate these options critically.

3.2.3 Sustain Dialogue

Learning is more likely to be cultivated when dialogue is ongoing. Continuous interaction helps actors develop deeper connections to the cultural, historical, and institutional contexts that drive environmental outcomes and better understand the underlying drivers of environmental issues (Nye, 1987). This process of deepening our understanding of complex issues is a form of "sensemaking." Sensemaking involves a continuous process of reorganizing, interpreting, and integrating different forms of information to view issues with greater complexity and nuance (Garrett et al., 2012).

A study comparing water management groups in Germany and Ireland found that when German water management groups had more opportunities and time to connect, participants learned more about each other than the Irish groups (Muro and Jeffrey, 2012). Similarly, in the UK, fisheries management groups with longer lifespans proved more likely to develop mutual trust, expand networks of collaboration, and produced higher problem-solving capabilities and more complex, reflexive learning (Garrett et al., 2012). Conversely, in the fisheries management groups characterized by weaker engagement and shorter lifespans, learning was more technical.

3.2.4 Pay Attention to Conflicts

Face-to-face dialogue can, at times, aggravate or create conflicts in the governance process, especially if not managed well. Conflict is not necessarily bad. It can be an opportunity for change and learning (Folke et al., 2005) especially when it heightens a sense of urgency for action. Conflicts also can lead people to reinforce or deepen their existing beliefs and perspectives and limit their learning from people with conflicting beliefs. For instance, a survey of people involved in climate and energy policy governance in the state of Colorado in the US found that those individuals with more extreme policy beliefs on climate and energy issues were more likely to reinforce their beliefs, rather than change them (Pattison, 2018).

Creating strategies to avoid the escalation of conflict, such as mediation or facilitation, can minimize the negative effects of conflict on learning in several ways. For instance, mediation can mitigate against intolerance, suspicion, and blame – all of which constrain receptiveness to different ideas across a group (Edmondson and Woolley, 2006) and discourage willingness to share or respect others' ideas. Even with good facilitation, productive dialogue with a large group of participants can be difficult. Building a governance process that can effectively manage conflict is not easy; it often requires establishing best practices and norms around dialogue at the outset (Stöhr and Chabay, 2014).

3.3 Nurturing Learning Leaders

Bringing people together in a learning process requires someone at the helm who can guide, inspire, and kick-start learning processes (Mahler, 1997). Leaders can also create an organizational culture that supports sharing information, a willingness to experiment, and a tolerance for error (Mahler, 1997; Lipshitz, et al., 2002). In terms of green infrastructure in Tucson, Arizona, learning was supported by engaging regularly with green infrastructure leaders nationally and through formalized learning circles. Leaders also nurtured other city departments, community organizations, and professional associations like landscapers. According to Blue Baldwin, Program Manager for Tucson's Storm to Shade program, sometimes this meant "breaking brains" by challenging old procurement or hiring processes at the city. "Sometimes you just have to shirk the status quo and be creative," says Blue. "I learned quickly that I couldn't just do things the old way. That would have gotten us nowhere."[3] The types of leaders that support learning usually are skilled in several areas. Although endless books have been written on leadership skills, here we draw out three types of skills often associated with learning leaders: innovation, facilitation, and brokering.

3.3.1 Spur Innovation

Learning leaders encourage creativity, challenge institutionalized knowledge, and actively disseminate innovative ideas from individuals to groups and organizations (Siebenhüner, 2008). Their leadership approach is often "transformative" – where they encourage others to question assumptions and look at old problems in new ways. Doing so enables people to adopt more generative and exploratory thinking processes and be more innovative and creative in problem solving (García-Morales et al., 2012).

Deeper forms of learning, which include both cognitive and behavioral change, demand leaders who are not afraid to build in processes within their organizations to promote learning (Siebenhüner, 2008). These processes encourage exploration, which involves risk taking and experimentation and requires feed-forward and feedback learning that challenges current institutionalized learning (Jansen et al., 2009). Leaders can initiate, promote, and support innovative approaches and strategies in a variety of ways. For example, an environmental agency director could bring in outside voices or plan activities outside the regular meeting space.

Community art is one emerging approach that leaders can support and guide to bring in more diverse interests and perspectives, and to communicate diverse narratives and knowledge in environmental governance spaces. Through "poetry routes" around river management, local communities in the Netherlands and Indonesia have been engaging in a facilitated arts-based process to produce and combine images and poems in a series of printed banners (Witteveen et al., 2022). The resulting poetry route then travels and creates spaces for dialogue with other stakeholders similarly concerned or engaged with the issue. Similarly, visual problem appraisal (VPA), a film-based learning strategy, involves sharing various perspectives through a series of filmed interviews. The diversity of filmed stories builds and unfolds through workshops, which requires leaders who can facilitate the storytelling

[3] Personal communication, November 18, 2022.

and enable stakeholders to hear other perspectives and examine conflicting interests. Photography and storytelling also have been used to facilitate sharing of Indigenous and local knowledge of marine issues in South Africa (Strand et al., 2022). With photovoice, participants were asked to take photographs using smartphones and then share photographs to engage discussions and dialogue between diverse stakeholders to help inform ocean governance processes. Leaders who can incorporate arts-based platforms into governance processes help others access and share alternative ways of understanding complex and dynamic systems and inspire people toward more creative ways to adapt to these changing conditions (Adler, 2006).

3.3.2 Facilitate

Learning leaders are skilled at facilitating and managing group processes in environmental governance (Imperial et al., 2016). Facilitation requires a wide range of techniques, such as asking questions, promoting inclusion, constructive discussions, practicing empathetic listening, recognizing power imbalances, managing tensions, and building better mutual understanding of interests and values (Fritz, 2021). Fundamentally, facilitation is "the art of surfacing, stimulating, and honing the creative tension within a group to help it move where it wants to go, needs to go, and how it wants to go" (Fierro, 2016: 33).

Facilitation skills matter for navigating through conflicts and communication challenges that inevitably arise when diverse people come together to solve environmental issues. Facilitation speeds up innovation and learning (Lubell et al., 2020). In various environmental governance processes, the presence of people with strong coordination and facilitation skills is often associated with better environmental outcomes (Olvera-Garcia and Neil, 2020).

In their study of moose management in Sweden, researchers highlighted the convening and facilitation role of leaders in the governance process (Dressel et al., 2021). Group members noted how facilitation assisted in providing a more balanced view from the various actors, including hunters and landowners, and helped to collect and share information key to learning. Participants spoke of the importance of functional meeting agendas to guide their work and contribute to more focused and meaningful discussions. Delegation of tasks helped harness the different strengths and expertise of the group members, cultivating an environment of inclusiveness. Participants acknowledged the role of leaders in championing the process and valued their flexibility and creativity in communication strategies and management tools.

3.3.3 Broker

Learning leaders are not always senior administrators or heads of organizations. Often, they are the individuals and organizations that make key connections in an environmental governance process – such as brokers or boundary spanners. They also include people who can formally facilitate the exchange of ideas in contentious contexts. To promote learning in environmental governance processes, such leaders often manage divergent stakeholder interests and navigate power differentials (Gerlak et al., 2020).

Leaders with brokering skills can support learning by facilitating communication across different groups and building shared meaning (Carlile, 2004). Brokers can aid decision-makers in acquiring and considering information that they would otherwise not obtain or incorporate in their decision-making (Michaels, 2009). Similarly, boundary-spanners can draw critical connections between disconnected groups in environmental governance. For instance, research on aquaculture partnerships found that when government actors play a leading role in the partnership, individuals in the partnership are more likely to learn (Resh et al., 2014).

Arizona State University's Decision Center for a Desert City (DCDC), which has brought scientists and policymakers together to collectively learn about and address specific issues for water governance, engaged in a variety of leadership practices (Crona and Parker, 2012). Their approach to reconciling competing demands required strategically timing engagement among different stakeholder groups within modeling workshops. When leaders felt a growing distrust in the decision model and the data on which it was based, DCDC leaders worked quickly to engage the workshop participants in a new round of discussion around the model and offered to customize and down-scale it to a level where it could be more useful to practitioners. A key player that they brought in – with credentials in both academia and in the water policy community – helped broker between different social spheres around the decision model. Another senior policy actor who served as a bridge between the water policy and the urban development community, provided critical linkages for water management in the region.

3.3.4 Avoid Over-Reliance on Traditional Leaders

Over-reliance on traditional leaders – or those established by their hierarchical position or power – can create barriers to learning (Pahl-Wostl et al., 2013). Leaders are not a panacea (Imperial et al., 2016), nor does leadership reside exclusively in one individual. By recognizing groups as sources of leadership (Uhl-Bien and Ospina, 2012) and using distributed leadership at various times in governance processes (Fitzsimons et al., 2011), an arsenal of strategies, skills, and approaches can be leveraged to promote learning (Imperial et al., 2016: 128–129). At the same time, the types of leadership needed for learning will depend on context-specific demands or skillsets of involved participants (Dressel et al., 2021).

Community members can also serve key roles in leading learning processes alongside professionals (Van de Kerkhof and Wieczorek, 2005). Researchers in Australia studied how community members participated in collaborative water planning processes in a water-scarce town in Victoria, Australia (Lindsay et al., 2019). Through an iterative process of workshops and focus groups over an eight-month period, project leaders brought together industry, government partners, and community members to develop a 50-year vision for the town. They found that community champions were able to challenge groupthink and question water professionals' assumptions and preconceived solutions.

3.4 Summary: Key Insights on Social Foundations

In this section, we identified foundational social features of environmental governance drawn from a preponderance of evidence in the learning scholarship. These features and their underlying mechanisms are summarized in Figure 4. The figure further helps visualize how the foundational social features interact and can support one another. Engaging diverse interests can be essential to fostering genuine dialogue and vice versa. But diversity can also lead to conflicts, which can be managed and improved through more genuine dialogue. Similarly, skilled learning leaders can play a key role in fostering genuine dialogue and engaging diverse interests. At the same time, engaging diverse interests can allow groups to identify more distributed forms of leadership that help avoid reliance on traditional leaders, and ideally help identify leaders with skills such as brokering. Instituting these

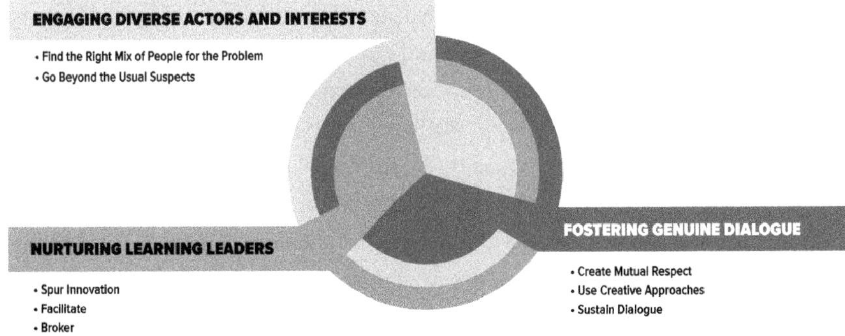

Figure 4 Foundational social features and mechanisms that support learning

social foundations does not guarantee learning. The extent to which these social features can enable learning, and how the features interact, depend on the structure of governance, which we examine in the following section.

4 The Structural Foundation for Learning

The social features of governance that support learning interact with the governance structures in which they take place (Bomberg, 2007). For instance, having a strong network structure that connects diverse actors can enable more effective information sharing, and help in the translation and dissemination of individual-level learning to collective learning. Governance structures can also ensure that procedures are in place for collective reflection (Mukhtarov et al., 2019), and can make learning intentional, and not merely ad hoc (Gerlak et al., 2020: 7).

For instance, how we organize monitoring and evaluation of environmental work structurally within a governance process can influence how we learn about and interpret governance effectiveness (e.g., da Silva Wells et al., 2013; Woodhill, 2019; Yanguas, 2021). One leading NGO – Oxfam – is experimenting with embedding mutual learning and exchange in its climate justice work in Africa. Through its work as a partner in a broader consortium-led project, titled African Activists for Climate Justice, Oxfam Nevib is working to strengthen civil society and advance solutions to the climate crisis in several African countries by helping to organize and mobilize women, youth, and Indigenous communities (AACJ, ND). To create structures for learning about the climate crisis, Oxfam is providing organizational resources, such as learning leaders, information systems, and strategies. Federico Costantini, who serves as the Mutual Capacity Strengthening Coordinator for Oxfam Novib, lives and breathes learning. "My job is to ensure that mutual learning and exchange takes places," remarks Costantini, "and I am finding lots of enthusiasm with the actors and communities around climate justice for learning."[4]

Oxfam is not alone in structuring governance processes to support learning. Based on research on other environmental governance actors and processes, we identify three main features that comprise the structural foundation for learning: (1) formalizing learning through feedback loops and learning venues, (2) allocating resources to learning, and (3) building learning networks. Like the social features identified in Section 3, structural features can be activated through multiple mechanisms, which we illustrate below. Again, these mechanisms may not represent all the ways to activate the structural foundations for learning. Rather, they offer a starting point for researchers interested in

[4] Personal communication, May 24, 2023.

developing learning theory and strategic leverage points for organizers of governance processes to intervene. Furthermore, these foundational structural features interact, are reinforcing, and shape the social features described in Section 3.

4.1 Formalizing Learning

One way to structure governance to facilitate learning is through formalized rules. Formalizing the stages of learning processes (acquiring, translating, and disseminating information) intentionally into the structure of governance can ensure that governance venues are more capable of deeper forms of learning, such as transformative learning (Wolfram, 2019; Gerlak et al., 2020). In the case of Oxfam, the organization embeds a dedicated learning person in each program for monitoring and evaluation. They pose learning questions over the course of a project connected to program objectives for climate justice. These learning questions help guide activities and direct end products. Most importantly, they provide a critical space for reflection. Increasingly, environmental governance actors like Oxfam are embracing structures that infuse feedback loops or adaptive management so that they improve future program design and implementation (e.g., Rijke et al., 2012; Chaffin et al., 2014). According to Carin Boersma, a global learning expert at Oxfam Novib, "everyone here wants to do more with learning. We are trying to build a learning culture. We want learning between units, within projects and across our projects. But we have to be careful that learning isn't abstract and not contextualized."[5]

4.1.1 Structure Venues for Learning

Formalizing learning means ensuring that venues for information sharing, knowledge building, and information dissemination are available. Learning-oriented venues can be found in policy labs that engage in experimentation and analysis (Lee and Ma, 2020), workshops aimed at building knowledge around uncertain or complex issues, collaborative working groups and teams, or task forces that bring together diverse groups or knowledge sources. For example, the South Florida Restoration Task Force, which oversees the Florida Everglades restoration planning and coordination that we introduced in Section 1 was organized to bring multiple federal and state agencies together with tribes. The goal was to learn about the complexities and challenges associated with the implementation of a multibillion-dollar restoration effort (Gerlak and Heikkila, 2011). In other ecosystem restoration programs, collaborative working

[5] Personal communication, July 25, 2023.

groups, such as California's Sacramento-San Joaquin Delta Interagency Ecological Program, similarly are designed as venues for intentional learning through collaborative monitoring and data synthesis by multiple agencies, NGOs, and scientists (Interagency Ecological Program, 2023).

Institutionalizing rules for diverse stakeholder participation or nontraditional forms of knowledge, especially in forums that traditionally are seen as "expert based" (Esguerra and van der Hel, 2021) can further support learning. Of course, formalizing or institutionalizing such participation directly influences the social characteristics of governance, described in Section 3, that are critical for learning. That formalization is not just about who has a seat at the table. Rules that mitigate power imbalances in information exchange, for instance, can be helpful for learning when diverse interests come together (Riche et al., 2020). Balancing formal rules with informal norms can further support the types of creative approaches we expect from learning leaders (Riche et al., 2020).

A project known as "Enhancing Livelihoods and Food Security from Agroforestry and Community Forestry in Nepal" (EnLiFT) offered a policy lab-like venue for integrating knowledge into forestry governance (Ojha et al., 2020). The project was established by the Nepalese government, Australian universities, and nongovernmental researchers in Nepal. The policy lab created a space to host events that focused on specific policy-related topics (e.g., clarifying the government-community contract for community forestry, scientific forest management, regulatory hurdles, land-use, and food security, among others). Each event brought together relevant participants knowledgeable about the issues – such as researchers, government agencies, various forestry-sector participants, donors, and politicians. Their learning outcomes included increased recognition of policy-related problems, identification of shared interests and concerns around private forestry, enhanced capacity for listening among conflicting policy actors, and policy change around timber harvesting. Researchers studying the project argue: "There is merit in going beyond the conventional forms of research dissemination to structure an iterative framework with which actors of science and policy can interact" (Ojha et al., 2020: 101997).

4.1.2 Establish Feedback Loops

As the previous example acknowledges, formalizing learning also requires learning feedback loops, which are common in adaptive management and planning. Adaptive management has been embraced in numerous environmental governance contexts, from the Glen Canyon Adaptive Management Program (Gerlak et al., 2021c) to governance of the Florida Everglades (Gunderson and Light,

2006) to the implementation of strategies for addressing water quality challenges under the European Union's Water Framework Directive (Kochskämper et al., 2021).

Adaptive management can be formalized through policy – as required under California's Delta Plan – to foster learning processes of planning, implementing, monitoring, and assessing management strategies (Delta Stewardship Council, 2023a). This approach is codified in state legislation (Delta Reform Act, 2009), which establishes adaptive management as "a framework and flexible decision-making process for ongoing knowledge acquisition, monitoring, and evaluation leading to continuous improvements in management planning and implementation" (California Water Code section 85052). Of course, the promise of adaptive management is not always realized in California's governance of water resources and ecosystems within the Delta (Delta Independent Science Board, 2016). Still, under this more formalized approach, the state has institutionalized an ongoing review of adaptive management (with advice from an Independent Science Board) and organizes regular adaptive management forums to support shared learning across stakeholders involved in or affected by adaptive management in the Delta (Delta Stewardship Council, 2023b).

At a more local level, projects for improving water quality in northern Germany have demonstrated that formalizing adaptive management can result in different types of learning – including both reducing ecological uncertainty and reducing social uncertainty about how stakeholders will respond to interventions (Kochskämper et al., 2021). More importantly, these adaptive management cases in Germany demonstrated that the "dual-feedback cycle" between ecological and social learning can be institutionalized. Doing so enables deeper forms of learning and facilitates the spread of lessons beyond a project to the broader governance system. Creating learning feedback loops across society and governance institutions can further support transitions toward more sustainable behaviors (Newell et al., 2022).

4.1.3 Enable Knowledge Co-production

Formalizing knowledge co-production that is inclusive of multiple types of actors who have direct experience with, or knowledge of an environmental governance issue can also support learning (Wyborn, 2015; Frantzeskaki & Kabisch, 2016; Zurba et al., 2022). Although knowledge co-production can occur in informal ways, more formalized approaches, such as through co-management structures or formal agreements are often key (Dale and Armitage, 2011). When historically marginalized governance actors are engaged in knowledge co-production, however, it can be important for such groups to have the agency to define their roles in the process and objectives (Turnhout et al., 2020).

In the Canadian Arctic, Indigenous groups, such as the Innuit and Innuvialuit, alongside different Canadian land and fisheries bodies, have established formal agreements to jointly manage fisheries and other resources (Armitage et al., 2011). One such case involved management of beluga whales that occasionally became trapped in ice. Initially, in the late 1980s, the Innuvialuit were treated as implementing parties and government officials were the decision-makers when dealing with this issue. This structure created barriers to knowledge sharing and learning. By the early 2000s stronger communication processes were institutionalized for understanding beluga entrapment problems. They encouraged Indigenous communities to share knowledge alongside government actors and build shared strategies for managing entrapment. The approach created long-term learning and enhanced capacity building for future beluga management.

4.1.4 Minimize Rigidity in Formal Structures

Formalizing learning can produce certain types of rigidity or blinders. For instance, creating formal feedback loops runs the risk of applying past lessons to future contexts that may not align with past experiences. This is called the overgeneralization trap (Beach and Smeets, 2022), or learning the wrong lessons.

At other times, we may build formalized processes that appear on the surface as mechanisms for learning, but in practice they are tools for reinforcing existing decisions or path dependencies. Consider environmental impact assessments and reviews as an example. These are tools that government agencies around the globe use to comply with national and subnational environmental impact laws when actions are proposed that could negatively harm the environment – like building new infrastructure. In theory these processes conduct extensive research and assessments on the potential risks, and sometimes benefits, of actions to issues like water quality, species habitat, air quality, and recreation access. These processes build in formal requirements for affected communities and other interest groups to comment on the draft impact statements to ensure that relevant impacts were assessed, and the analytical approach was reasonable. Yet, such tools at their worst often are rubber stamps for proposed actions. At their best, they can lead to changes in the design of actions and sometimes stop actions – which can be indicative of learning. But without strong stakeholder engagement, transparency, and dialogue around the process – such learning is less likely (Nita et al., 2022).

At the same time, informal exchanges offer the potential for more personal and meaningful engagement that fosters learning (Sattler and Schroter, 2022). In other words, the formal structures need to align with the principles that we described in Section 3. As Riche and colleagues (2020: 12) argue, learning is more effective in governance processes when informal norms allow for creativity, but also when formal rules allow for adequate information exchange. Formalizing learning may be necessary to overcome some of the risks of relying too much on processes that could be subject to the whims of the next leader, or the personalities of people involved. But building in too much rigidity into the process through formal procedures can hinder opportunities for social learning and genuine engagement (Pahl-Wostl et al., 2007a).

4.2 Allocating Learning Resources

In addition to formalizing learning, governance structures need resources to spark learning processes and sustain them. These resources may be internal to a decision-making venue or process (e.g., financial, and technical resources) or external to the process. External resources include laws and policies that enable or support these internal resources. The scale and scope of the people and governance activities involved will create different resource needs, and context-specific capacity features should be diagnosed and assessed to identify what resources might enable or hinder learning (Wolfram, 2019; Gerlak et al., 2020: 8). At the same time, environmental issues that are emerging in the future often involve deep uncertainty – or the unknowns that extend beyond our capacity to predict or expect with the standard information sources (e.g., government agency monitoring and scientific modeling) (Marchau et al., 2019). As a result, environmental governance actors also need to dedicate resources for learning about the types of futures that are difficult to predict – such as through horizon scanning or robust decision-making, where current strategies can be stress-tested according to a range of possible future conditions.

Learning resources also should be transparent and explicit. For instance, in the African Activists for Climate Justice Program, Oxfam Novib is advancing a capacity assessment tool to help systematize learning within the larger program. This involves Oxfam Novib co-creating with partners a set of topics and issue areas of interest to the partners. Through a platform approach, these topics of interest, from participatory action research methods and financial management to partnership building, are shared. Partners in the program offer their skills to support the broader network but then also draw from the expertise of others. Resources can then be deployed to fund the specific requests or help engage in new targeted areas of work through a small grants program. "This is really key to shifting the narrative around development from the Global North being the expert to a new way to think about capacity development that more broadly shares the strengths of all members of the broader consortium," according to Costantini.[6]

4.2.1 Invest in Novel Sources of Information

Often one of the barriers to learning stems from our tendency toward confirmation biases, status quo biases, and desirability biases in decision-making, as we discussed in Section 1. However, governance can be structured to help overcome these biases and think creatively. For instance, learning can be enhanced in governance structures that facilitate the active pursuit of novel sources of information (Bodin et al., 2006; Bodin, 2017). These tools, such as scenario planning, can mitigate cognitive biases and build openness to innovative ideas (Haasnoot et al., 2018; Ward et al., 2024). They also can include methods that explicitly assess the disparity between what is known and what needs to be known for a responsible decision (Ben-Haim, 2019).

The Global Governance Project studied learning in eight international organizations with a focus on international environmental policy over more than a 10-year period. It focused on the role of learning mechanisms, such as independent evaluation reports, expert workshops, and project reviews. Researchers found these mechanisms helped acquire new knowledge and implement solutions to organizational problems (Siebenhüner, 2008). When international organizations, like the World Bank and UNEP, scanned both the internal and external environment, they were better prepared to trigger more reflexive learning than those that closed off their organization against such knowledge. Dedicating resources to novel information also enabled foundational social features, which we described in the previous section that can support learning – namely diverse forms of engagement between stakeholders, staff members, and external experts. And their learning resulted in rethinking the environmental impacts of the Bank's operations and supported modifications to lending policies and the internal culture of the World Bank.

4.2.2 Borrow from Your Neighbors

Another way that resources can be allocated to support learning, especially in resource constrained environments, is by borrowing knowledge or lessons from similar governance venues or processes. When we first studied learning in the

[6] Personal communication, May 24, 2023.

Everglades, we heard that leaders of the restoration effort were hungry to learn how other types of large-scale ecosystem restoration efforts across the US were grappling with similar challenges. Learning about governance strategies in similar contexts can be supported by strong networks, as we discuss in more detail below. Learning from neighbors may require dedicated staff or technology that can help track and identify which types of governance actors are engaged in or facing similar challenges, while also putting resources into creating the space and time for conversations and lesson sharing.

For instance, in a study of hurricane recovery in Gulf of Mexico communities, task teams with outside experts with recent memory of major storms were important for planning, securing funding, and implementing recovery (Dunning, 2020). These experts helped fill knowledge gaps and enabled successful planning and competitive applications for federal aid. Similarly, in their study of noise pollution at airports, researchers in the Netherlands highlight the notion of "transnational communication" where countries learn from the environmental policies of other countries (Veenman and Liefferink, 2014: 156). Countries learned through informal mechanisms like phone calls but also from other countries working to mitigate noise pollution through more formalized meetings. In Germany, different federal states learned from each other about how best to design participatory flood risk planning (Newig et al., 2016). Lessons sourced from other jurisdictions or policy fields can spur such learning by providing inspiration.

4.2.3 Dedicate Capacity, at the Right Time and Place

Fostering and maintaining learning resources also requires dedicated capacity to strategically deploy those resources. Examples of this capacity include experts and technical resources for information management and analysis (Lagadec, 1997), legal and policy guidance, and resources for convening and sustaining the type of dialogue we identified in Section 3. Such resources are particularly critical if decision-makers or leaders of governance venues and programs are serious about connecting with actors who bring Indigenous knowledge and TEK or environmental justice perspectives. As we know from experts who study public participation processes (e.g., Fung, 2015), simply expecting that nongovernmental actors will show up and have time to engage in dialogue can be naïve. And worse, such expectations can reinforce past inequities if it is costly for historically marginalized actors to engage. Participating in governance takes time and compensating people who engage outside of their regular professional roles can be critical to ensuring that their capacity exists to be part of learning processes. This capacity can be structured within the strategic goals of governance actors and in their approaches to crafting, implementing, monitoring, and enforcing policies and programs.

Research on environmental disasters and crises has reinforced the importance of dedicating key resources in support of learning. Crow and Albright's (2019) study of communities that were severely impacted by massive flooding in Colorado's Front Range found that deeper forms and more deliberative forms of learning in recovery efforts appeared in communities that had both strong resource flows – from financial, technical, and human resources – and strong collaborative relationships to higher levels of government. Although learning may be constrained when financial resources are limited (Taylor et al., 2023), there are ways to allocate nonfinancial resources for those critical times when learning capacity needs to ramp up (Ricco and Schultz, 2019).

4.2.4 Sidestep Resource Constraints

There is no question that resources for learning will be constrained in every environmental governance context. As a result, leaders of governance organizations or programs might be more interested in investing in resources targeted for mission-critical activities rather than toward those that support learning. Regardless of the perception or the reality of resource constraints, targeted action can be directed to support learning. Recognizing how learning is key to supporting mission-critical activities or outcomes could be the first step. Utilizing tools for learning that might be less resource intensive, borrowing resources from partners in networks (as we discuss in more detail below), and targeting resources towards key actors or actions that are known to foster learning can further help overcome resource constraints (Gerlak et al., 2020: 8).

In line with experience from the COVID-19 pandemic, using lower-cost structures such as online platforms, to support the type of dialogue described in the last section is one approach to mitigate resource constraints. Andrade et al. (2023) facilitated a series of online deliberative engagements for local stakeholders from Interior Alaska to discuss landscape change and associated management practices. Using the online forums helped identify shared values and spark value shifts across stakeholder groups. Despite some potential limitations with online forums, their use lowered participation costs for people who might have to travel long-distances and allowed for more diverse viewpoints to be brought into environmental decision-making. Virtual spaces, however, may not be appropriate for more reflexive learning, which requires thoughtful structuring of communication norms. Other approaches might also help overcome resource constraints. For instance, we might be able to use AI to compile lessons on how other decision makers are enabling learning. This could include looking for publicly available information on forums that incorporate diverse stakeholder dialogue, or searching for examples of creative stakeholder engagement, or finding insights on leadership training programs that incorporate learning skills.

4.3 Building Learning Networks

Building formalized learning structures and allocating adequate resources target more internal structural features of governance. These investments and actions can help to strengthen internal bonds that build trust and create shared social norms (Newman and Dale, 2005). Those structures and resources also need to be networked with diverse types of actors, as discussed in Section 3. In environmental governance, the cross-scale nature of environmental problems means that the networks across and within various governing structures are essential for learning (Pahl-Wostl et al., 2007b). Creating connections across different organizations and venues can ensure that learning is hard-wired across the system. The network established through the African Activists for Climate Justice project involves some 60 organizations operating at diverse levels from grassroots to regional and transnational organization efforts. Building this network and strengthening capacity is central to program objectives and success. The network tries to coordinate and amplify the voices of these organizations. According to Costantini, "The biggest benefit I see is the exchange between partners across countries and in the same countries. Our work supports partners in working together, perhaps developing strategies, and for sure it strengthens the networks that exist but also create new ones."[7]

4.3.1 Create Multilevel Scaffolding

Governance networks need to be well-connected across multiple levels of actors and venues to support learning (Crona and Parker, 2012; Resh et al., 2014; Gerlak et al., 2020: 7). Broad reaching networks that cross diverse types of actors and positions can facilitate information sharing and knowledge access and production (Newig et al., 2010; Heikkila and Gerlak, 2013: 496). Learning can also be fostered when multilevel networks align around shared goals (Armitage et al., 2011) and establish communication pathways across levels, from individuals to organizations (Crossan et al., 1999). Such connections further need to ensure that actors have adequate access to novel sources of information and knowledge (Bodin et al., 2006; Bodin, 2017). Such networks

[7] Personal communication, May 24, 2023.

cannot be developed haphazardly. Tailoring them to the functional purpose of a governance system can be important for learning (Rijke et al., 2012).

One example of how multilevel networks facilitate collective learning is the Communities Committee of the Seventh American Forest Congress, where forestry leaders and stakeholders come together to discuss US forest policy issues (Cheng et al., 2011). The Communities Committee started in 1996, although the Forest Congress has been in place since 1882. The Communities Committee is an open membership group focused on fostering forest stewardship and has worked with other nongovernmental forestry groups to inform federal forestry policy. They also help community forestry practitioners learn about various tactics and strategies for working with the federal government and identify opportunities for community-based forestry, while providing learning opportunities for federal elected officials about community forestry.

4.3.2 Include Boundary Spanning Partners

Many boundaries are often at play in environmental governance including land ownership, functional management tasks, organizational missions and cultures, and even different individual and organizational conceptions of and knowledge of environmental matters (Davis et al., 2021: 4). Spanning these boundaries is important in fostering resilience and adaptive governance within social-ecological systems (Quick and Feldman, 2014; Newell et al., 2022). Particularly in governance settings with a wide variety of fragmented actors and venues, boundary organizations can create strategic bridges between actors who do not have opportunities to interact or who work in vastly different domains (Sattler and Schroter, 2022). These bridges foster learning when new relationships and shared knowledge are built (O'Mahony and Bechky, 2008; Fischer, 2015). Boundary organizations also can drive knowledge co-production and integration of diverse knowledge into policymaking and practice (Guston, 2001; Crona and Parker, 2012; Feldman and Ingram, 2009). To do this, boundary organizations may need to create and utilize boundary objects, which take up concrete or actionable forms like maps, models, scenarios, or reports, agreements, and shared data (Davis et al., 2021: 8).

In the early 2000s, a Field School in the Waorani and Achuar communities in the Ecuadorian Amazon was created to provide employment and to capitalize on opportunities to generate revenue from the educational tourism industry (Buzinde et al., 2020). The Field School serves as a boundary organization comprised of members representing academic institutions and members of Indigenous communities. The role of this boundary organization is to work cross-culturally to build diverse networks that are based on trust and respect and can enhance adaptive capacity through knowledge exchange and learning. Through the program, locals teach the local language and bio culture to Western students who pay to get immersed in local knowledge systems related to sustainability. Boundary objects are used to acquaint non-Indigenous people with local Indigenous perspectives and include videos that capture key aspects of Indigenous knowledge. Games, as discussed in Section 3, can also serve as boundary objects helping to facilitate shared learning and collaboration between stakeholders.

4.3.3 Understand the Tradeoffs of Different Network Structures

Networks vary in terms of their structure and actor composition, which impose different strengths and weaknesses for learning (Rijke, 2012). Especially in complex governance settings, network structures that limit interactions between different subgroups can impede learning (Bodin, 2017). In these situations, learning may be restricted to the concerns and ideas of those who are most powerful (Schusler et al., 2003; Roome and Wijen, 2006). Although more connectivity or density across a network may allow more opportunities to acquire information and learn quickly, excessively dense networks can also produce more homogenous information and impede learning (Rijke et al., 2012).

Similarly, networks with highly centralized actors can enhance information flows, but they may also constrain diversity of input and deeper levels of learning (Bodin et al., 2006). In the case of the Venice canal system, a highly hierarchical and centralized governance system that lacked connectivity resulted in closed coalitions, and limited communication and knowledge sharing, which made policy change difficult (Munaretto and Huitema, 2012). Conversely, networks with less centrality may facilitate broader engagement and shared learning (Henry, 2009), but may increase the transaction costs of learning processes (Gerlak and Heikkila, 2011).

Furthermore, there is a tendency for people to form networks with people they share beliefs with, or bonding ties, and the boundaries of such a network create constraints on learning (Henry and Vollan, 2014). While people may be more likely to trust information coming from people who share similar beliefs, homogeneity of actors in networks may constrain the diversity of ideas and impede learning (Newig et al., 2010). This is because more homogeneous governance structures – that is, intra-sectoral networks – may not allow for the type of "bridging" ties that are needed for knowledge acquisition (Dow et al., 2013). When people build governance networks around shared beliefs, learning may be focused on reinforcing existing beliefs (Weible et al., 2023).

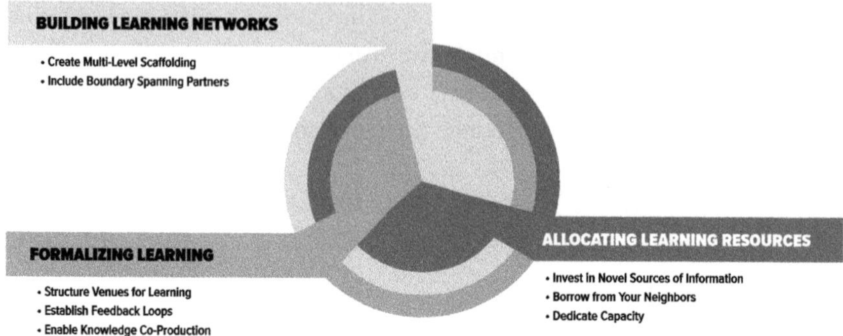

Figure 5 Foundational structural features and mechanisms that support learning

A "dynamic interplay" of bridging and bonding links, which serve to build more internal trust and norms, may be needed to promote learning to support environmental governance (Newman and Dale, 2005).

4.4 Summary of Structural Foundations

In this section, the structural foundations are based on where we see a preponderance of evidence from learning scholarship describing structural features and mechanisms that support learning. As illustrated in Figure 5, these structural features and the mechanisms reinforce each other. Formalizing learning structures and building learning networks are more likely to be feasible when learning resources are allocated, for instance. The extent to which these structural features are effective in spurring learning, however, may depend on how well the social elements of governance, as described in Section 3, function. In Section 5, we bring together insights about both the social and structural features and what steps both practitioners and researchers can take to diagnose and support them.

5 Infusing Learning into Environmental Governance

Learning about the drivers of environmental problems and about the strategies and policies that can mitigate them can help us adapt to changing environmental conditions. Learning intentionally and reflexively can support governance choices that are better informed and suited to the complex environmental challenges we face. When governance processes are designed for learning, they are also more likely to achieve societal goals of improving equity and justice in environmental governance. At least, these are the assumptions of the learning hypothesis for environmental governance.

But learning is hard. In environmental governance processes, people may be resistant to learning certain types of information. Or decision-making bodies may learn about and prioritize a limited scope of information – often from those who hold the greatest power or most resources. Resistance to learning arises not just around the technical and biophysical issues driving environmental governance problems. Such resistance becomes more intense when governance actors are faced with learning about the values and priorities of people and organizations who drive these problems, are affected by them, or bear responsibility for solving them.

As most environmental governance systems involve complex sets of actors, venues, and issues, governance actors must confront competing values and interests to understand and solve environmental problems. When people with fundamentally different viewpoints engage in a governance process, their cognitive biases can be triggered or reinforced. These cognitive biases restrict how different individuals access and interpret information. They also constrain how willing individuals are to learn. At the same time, even when governance actors learn, not all learning is productive or aligned well with the demands of decision-makers. As a result, there are many ways learning can be constrained or even blocked from influencing governance outcomes. The result is that learning in environmental governance can often be idiosyncratic and reactive. Without taking the time to build learning into governance intentionally, governance actors lack capacity to learn productively and connect learning to our governance processes and solutions.

Despite the constraints on learning, productive forms of learning in environmental governance are happening across the globe. From city officials in Tucson, Arizona working on green infrastructure to an NGO engaged in climate justice in Africa, environmental governance practitioners are actively working to infuse learning into governance processes and decisions. At the same time, scholars of environmental governance are increasingly interested in examining how learning emerges, what supports or impedes it, and what it leads to. Yet, decision-makers are building learning processes in venues around the world in isolation from one another, and researchers are studying and assessing those cases in isolation. As a result, prior research has not offered a strong understanding of the social and structural features of governance that can support more intentional learning, or clear pathways to overcome some of the key barriers to learning. Equally challenging is that with so many different definitions and approaches to learning, it is easy to get lost in the weeds when assessing learning. The goal of this Element is to bring rich empirical and theoretical insights together to distill and synthesize lessons on how researchers and practitioners can better understand, diagnose, and support learning in environmental governance.

5.1 Summary of Key Insights and Caveats

A core message of this Element is that to infuse learning in environmental governance, it must be done intentionally. Being intentional about learning begins with recognizing the value in learning as a tool to improve environmental governance. It then requires communicating this value broadly in governance settings (e.g., the venues, decision-making processes, or organizations involved in governance). Intentionality also emphasizes the importance of choosing words carefully to signal what learning means and why it matters. For researchers, being able to study and evaluate intentional learning further requires clarity in how learning is defined and conceptualized. Intentionality further calls for a commitment by practitioners and scholars to collectively reflect on the work being done and an openness to experimentation to build, and even rebuild, the social and structural features of environmental governance.

In Sections 1 and 2, we offer a straightforward approach to help researchers, students, and practitioners establish shared understanding of learning in environmental governance. This approach builds upon extensive theoretical and empirical examples across the learning scholarship. As we acknowledge earlier, learning in environmental governance starts with individual cognitive learning, but goes beyond it. It involves a collective process of acquiring, translating, and disseminating new knowledge, ideas, or information, along with collective products such as changes to beliefs or behaviors by governance actors. To help unpack and detect learning, we also highlight how looking for who learns, how they learn, where they learn, what they learn, and to which effect, are key starting points. These questions can disentangle the complexities of collective learning, the depths of learning, and what might drive it in different governance contexts.

The diversity of case studies we draw upon in Sections 3 and 4, along with our own research over the past two decades, provide fruitful insights into how we can foster learning and mitigate some of the barriers to learning. Specifically, we identify several social and structural features of governance – which we call the foundations of learning. The social foundation includes fostering diverse interests, engaging in genuine dialogue, and nurturing learning leaders, while the structural foundation includes formalizing learning, allocating learning resources, and building learning networks. The mechanisms that allow these foundational features to emerge vary by feature and may vary by the type of governance setting or broader context. That is, we cannot interpret the social and structural foundations, or the mechanisms that drive them, as discrete items of a checklist. There is no singular approach to learning. Each governance venue, decision-making process, or organization involved will have different capacities for learning and experiences with learning. And each environmental governance problem or proposed solution we face will have varying knowledge bases, complexity, and urgency.

Digging into how the foundational features and their mechanisms trigger learning might point us down a long chain of causal pathways where we begin to see other fundamental governance characteristics that are important for learning. For instance, when we consider the foundational features of genuine dialogue and skilled learning leaders, we see that their presence can also foster a sense of trust in other governance actors or in the process. We acknowledge that trust can play a key role in environmental governance learning (Pahl Wostl et al., 2007a; Reed, 2008; Leach et al., 2014; Ernst, 2019), and plays a key role in learning in various organizational and social contexts (Edmondson, 2004; Koole, 2020). We addressed the role of distrust as a barrier in Section 1, and the ways in which trust intersects with various social and structural features of governance in Sections 3 and 4. However, we did not focus on trust as a foundational feature for learning. In part, this is because the role of trust is complex and may go beyond learning. For instance, it can serve as a secondary mechanism that arises when one of the other learning mechanisms is triggered (Ernst, 2019). In addition, it is foundational to other governance processes – such as fostering collective action, conflict resolution, and collaborative governance (e.g., see Leach and Sabatier, 2005; Ostrom, 2009; Berardo and Schultz, 2010; Bodin et al, 2020). These processes are beyond the scope of this Element. That said, it would be naïve to ignore trust. It might be a necessary, but not sufficient, mechanism of governance effectiveness more broadly (which includes the capacity for learning), which we will continue to grapple with.

We recognize that certain foundational governance features that support learning may be more feasible, while others may be less so, depending on the governance setting. Creative approaches for fostering genuine dialogue, for instance, have been discussed in practice and theory for decades, but such approaches can be hard to implement. They require taking risks. Given the bureaucratic structure and legalistic approaches that are baked into many environmental governance processes, risk taking is rare. Yet, if designed well, novel approaches like storytelling, or using art, or serious games can help people take abstract forms of knowledge and bring them meaning and vitality, often by connecting ideas to individuals' lived experiences (Tandon et al., 2016). Finding ways to overcome bureaucratic resistance to creative approaches might require strong leadership, dedicated learning resources, and structures that help governance leaders identify creative approaches for inspiration. Again, the foundational social and structural features and mechanisms can play a key role in reinforcing each other in support of learning. In addition, how they work together will depend not only on the governance setting, but also on the broader context (e.g., biophysical, socio-economic, or institutional). The characteristics of broader governance contexts shape what governance actors pay attention to, influencing the scope of learning and capacity to adapt the social and structural features of governance.

Figure 6 provides a graphic illustration of how these foundational features of governance intersect with the defining elements of governance, and how they feedback into the governance setting and broader context. This helps to shed

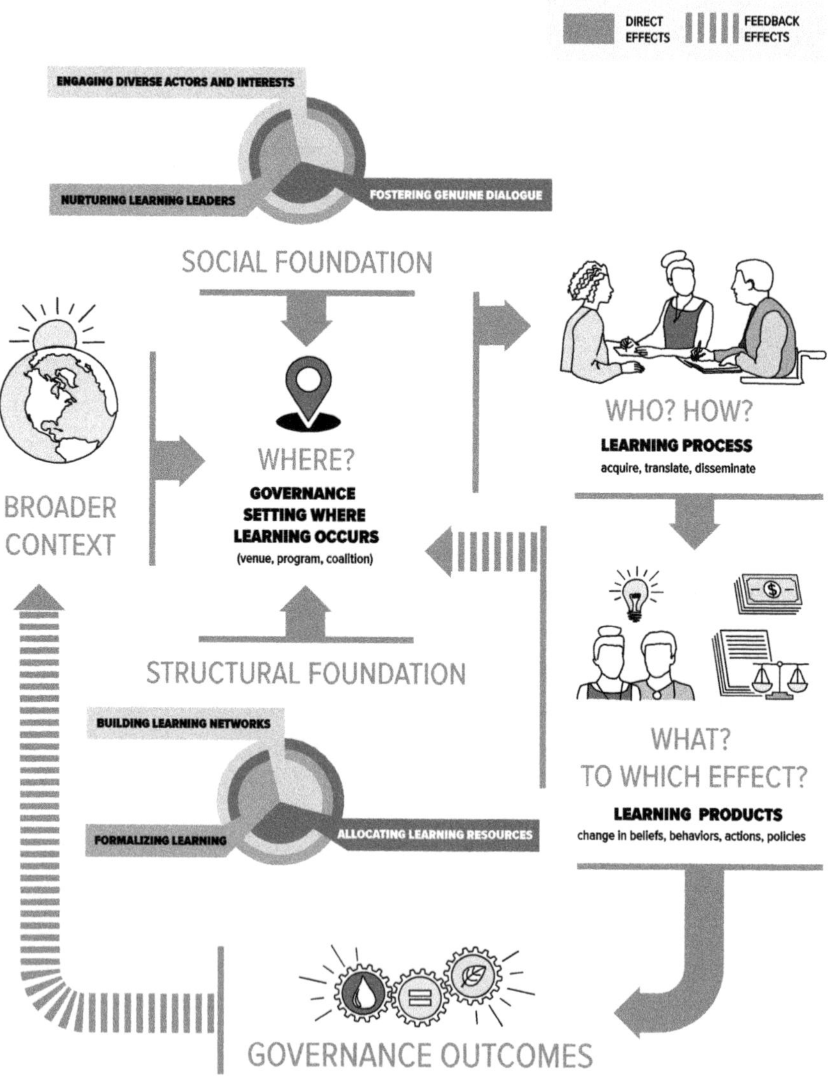

Figure 6 Diagnosing learning in environmental governance

light on critical interactions and linkages across the social and structural features. Together they highlight the core features that can guide diagnoses of learning, which we describe in more detail below.

At the same time, we highlighted several caveats to consider when implementing the foundational features in Sections 3 and 4, which acknowledge how tradeoffs and sometimes unintended consequences can arise when changing or adapting governance processes or structures to spur learning. These caveats included:

- Watch out for pitfalls when engaging diverse interests,
- Pay attention to conflicts,
- Avoid over-reliance on traditional leaders,
- Minimize rigidity in formal structures,
- Sidestep resource constraints, and
- Understand the tradeoffs of different network structures.

5.2 Taking a Diagnostic Approach to Learning

Being attentive to the caveats discussed in Sections 3 and 4 reminds us that intentional learning requires continuous diagnoses of learning, and interventions to improve learning. That is, we may need to regularly assess the extent to which governance settings support learning. We then need to use that information to design and redesign governance processes and anticipate potential pitfalls. We rarely get a chance to design policy or governance processes from scratch. Instead, we must tweak and reshape existing ones to adapt to changing environmental, social, and political circumstances.

Similarly, researchers are often studying venues and governance arrangements with deep histories and past interactions. Through a diagnostic approach, practitioners can more intentionally assess how to adapt the social and structural foundations needed for learning as organizational and political contexts change. Regularly doing so can further become part of an institutionalized norm for learning. Likewise, researchers can provide analytic support – through rigorous methodologies for assessing and diagnosing learning. They also can draw comparisons across multiple types of governance processes, organizations, and systems to update knowledge of the governance features and mechanisms that work better in different settings.

Of course, not all the foundational features outlined in Sections 3 and 4 are necessary for every situation. Some might be more important or more feasible given resource constraints or the political environment. One could imagine a government agency that recognizes it has good access to internal knowledge about how its ecosystem restoration programs are working. Yet, it struggles with accessing external networks and diverse sources of information from agencies around the world doing similar work to better inform its work. Or there might be an environmental NGO struggling to develop learning capacity within the communities where it works because it lacks opportunities for genuine dialogue. Or a private company that must comply with environmental regulations might recognize how limited their engagement is with the relevant stakeholders, which then impedes their capacity for learning about effective strategies for regulatory compliance. Conversely, there may be new opportunities – in terms of resources, leadership, or new partnerships – that can be targeted directly to support learning. To help infuse such learning into environmental governance through a diagnostic approach, we offer two strategies: (1) ask learning questions; and (2) set learning triggers.

5.2.1 Ask Learning Questions

Researchers and practitioners can start by using the social and structural features and mechanisms from Sections 3 and 4 to diagnose where learning in governance settings can be enhanced. Through a diagnostic approach, we can better assess how to adapt the social and structural elements of governance needed for learning, particularly as organizational and political contexts change. This involves introducing the concept of learning and then examining the processes used in a specific governance venue, decision-making process, or organization. You can begin by asking if any of the social or structural foundational features of learning exist.

- *Which of the social and structural features are present;*
- *What is missing; and*
- *How are foundational features interacting?*

Furthermore, guiding questions outlined in Section 2 can be posed about who learns, how learning occurs, where people learn, what they learn, and to which effect. Doing so can make learning processes and products more visible (e.g., as highlighted in Figure 6). From there, it is easier to draw connections between the indicators of learning and the social and structural features of governance we would expect to support learning (also shown in Figure 6).

In diagnosing how learning occurs, consider whether different collective learning stages are activated (i.e., acquisition, translation, and dissemination of information). As we described in Section 2, even if individuals are learning on their own, learning for environmental governance cannot be triggered without a collective learning process. That means governance actors intentionally seek out new ideas, interpret, and disseminate that information across groups, organizations, and networks. Asking whether and how learning processes are enabled will also point out where, or which governance processes, might need investments in the foundational features described above. In some cases, learning processes can be enhanced by a stronger social foundation, like engaging diverse actors and interests, fostering genuine dialogue, and nurturing skilled learning leaders. In other cases, deeper structural change might be needed to spark learning. Key questions to ask might be:

- *Is a new collaborative body needed to bring diverse actors together;*
- *Where could resources be directed to build greater capacity; and*
- *What kind of networks are desirable to achieve the types of learning outcomes that will help advance governance goals?*

5.2.2 Set Learning Triggers

A second pathway to infuse learning into environmental governance is to establish triggers for when and how we diagnose learning. Paying attention to notable moments of learning or non-learning from past actions can help diagnose what governance changes could support learning in the future. This might mean looking at timelines of planned programs or policy implementation efforts and devising a "learning summit" at key points in the process. Through dialogue and reflection, actors in a particular governance setting can then undertake a formal diagnosis of past actions. Again, using the tools from Section 2 to analyze the who, how, what, to which effect, and where of learning is key to the diagnosis. Such assessments can allow actors to identify where learning blockages might be occurring (e.g., who is holding up the flow of information and why), or where the social foundation may be incomplete or lacking. Conversely, it can reveal the presence of mechanisms, such as learning leaders or networks, which supported learning or contributed to blocked learning or non-learning in past actions.

We can also look to examples where environmental policies or programs have failed to meet key goals and use such examples to trigger learning processes. Failures are often instructive because they focus attention on problems that can build new knowledge about what to do differently in the future (McConnell, 2015; Sokolowski and Heffron, 2022). However, due to our negativity bias, we can over-learn or focus too intently on our failures as triggers for learning, potentially ignoring important lessons from cases of success (Beach and Smeets, 2022). Considering policy successes – or at least cases that are not deemed as failures – can further infuse learning into governance. For example, an appreciative inquiry approach encourages organizations to identify what is working well in their organization and envision how to make positive outcomes occur more frequently (Fam et al., 2013). With this approach, problems are reframed to focus on strengths and successes by asking participants to identify what works well, why it works well, and what they want to see more of in their organization (Coghlan et al., 2003). Another approach is a premortem, which occurs before a project or effort is launched, and through a hypothetical asks the participants to explain the reasons why the effort might fail to anticipate and head off future problems (Klein, 2007: Smerek, 2018).

Like the tools of program evaluation and policy analysis, being able to assess different governance outcomes, and understand the drivers of those outcomes creates a formalized process for learning. It embeds regularized acquisition of information into governance, ensuring that processes are in place to formally assess and interpret that information. Whether the lessons from that process result in changes into the design of future policy or governance depends on how well the social and structural foundations of learning are established.

5.3 Embracing a Learning Mindset

To enable more open and regular diagnostic approaches to intentional learning, practitioners and researchers can promote a learning mindset when engaging in or assessing governance processes. A learning mindset starts by adopting a common orientation, or shared language of learning across governance actors. It also includes building a shared motivation and willingness to learn (Velardi et al., 2021). It is about creating spaces where people are excited to learn and able to share what they have learned. Because reflection is a cognitive skill, developing the capacity to reflect demands practice and feedback (Barnett, 1995). Doing so creates psychological safety so people feel comfortable sharing failures and lessons. Embracing these features of a learning mindset can foster the social and organizational norms that encourage learning (Smerek, 2018: 16).

These norms can help prepare governance actors for adapting the social and structural features of governance described above and encourage open experimentation with redesigning our institutions. Such experimentation is akin to "learning to learn" – and making learning an ongoing effort. "Learning to learn" requires sensitivity to how alternative types of learning may be needed for given circumstances. It also means paying attention to how different social and structural features might be more effective at key stages of learning processes. For example, structuring governance for acquiring information might be different from disseminating information and knowledge. Or learning about social systems might require more emphasis on genuine dialogue than learning about technical matters, which may require more dedication to key learning resources.

To capture these nuances means assessing indicators of learning and establishing learning feedback loops to improve when we are not on the right path. At the same time, too much experimentation can create fear and organizational resistance among governance actors. Balancing flexibility built into learning systems with organizational consistency on issues such as accountability, can be critical for long-term resilience in environmental governance (Beunen et al., 2017).

Learning-by-doing is another important aspect of developing the learning mindset and capacity. Practitioners can deploy learning-relevant skills or actions and then reflect on them (Senge, 1990). They can also do dry-runs or simulations of activities that can create a safe space for reflection, promoting psychological safety among team members (Edmondson, 2004: 252). Or practitioners can embrace a café approach that helps groups engage in constructive dialogue, build personal relationships, and foster collaborative learning (Tan and Brown, 2005). Creating learning spaces where participants can interact, develop shared experiences, and establish trust (Johnson and Wilson, 2009) are pathways to a learning mindset.

Finally, a learning mindset needs to be regularized and sustained over time (Schusler et al., 2003; Gerlak et al., 2020). Learning takes time to manifest. It cannot be seen as *ad hoc* or approached as a one-off exercise. And formal processes may not always sustain learning. Learning needs to be part of the informal norms and processes in governance settings, especially when the formal approaches are lacking. To do this may require revisiting the social and structural features that can support a learning system and assessing how well they work or whether they need to be adapted. It won't be easy. Genuine learning can be inhibited by a lack of institutional self-reflection within dominant science and policy organizations (Pallett and Chilvers, 2013). We need to guard against the political strategies, social biases, or dominant discourses that work against cultivating reflexivity or engaging in social change (Stoddart and Atlin, 2022). That also means guarding against assuming that the insights in this Element are set in stone.

5.4 Connecting Research to Practice

Our recommendations for using a diagnostic approach and embracing a learning mindset are, we hope, useful for advancing not only how we assess, but how we practice learning in environmental governance. We see them as valuable for guiding both practitioners engaged in environmental governance and academics studying environmental governance and helping connect research to practice. For our colleagues whose interests are more academic, the diagnostic approach presented above could guide some of the approaches that are most fruitful when studying learning, particularly if researchers are able to rely on practitioners' own diagnoses for insights on understanding where and when learning is most challenging. Researchers may have the capacity to study such challenges more deeply or bring teams together to compare and assess learning processes and products across different governance processes. In doing so, the diagnostic approach might help researchers start to tackle questions that commonly plague learning research through a different lens. Questions such as *when* does conflict help support learning; *where* is learning more likely to be blocked; *whose* interests and knowledge are most likely to be reflected in collective learning; and *what* is produced through collective learning remain under-studied in learning research. Likewise when practitioners build a learning mindset into governance processes, this can create a sense of openness and willingness to co-learn with researchers who might bring valuable analytical skills to enable regularized diagnoses of learning.

Additionally, the foundational elements and their mechanisms from Sections 3 and 4 – offer empirically-grounded expectations about what governance factors support learning. These expectations need ongoing testing across diverse types of environmental governance settings and iteration between learning theories and practice. That is, the academic community interested in learning should also be regularly assessing and re-evaluating the accuracy, validity, and strength of our assumptions and hypotheses, and our theoretical evidence. By focusing on social and structural foundations of governance that support learning, we may have missed other features of governance that can shape learning. Our own framework on learning (Heikkila and Gerlak, 2013), for example, highlights how events exogenous to the governance setting, such as crises can spur learning. Looking at those exogenous events driving key environmental challenges will undoubtedly be important for learning researchers. For instance, will certain types of climate change driven events – like melting ice sheets or sea level rise – trigger more rapid learning on how we govern climate change?

Relatedly, our framework also has discussed how the technological and functional domain of a governance setting can affect learning, which we did not explore in depth in this Element. For example, the complexity of environmental issues and what tools exist to help us monitor them or disseminate information can shape learning. One of the challenges for studying learning may be the extent to which rapid advances in knowledge system, with the support of AI, makes it more (or less) feasible for governance actors to learn, especially about new and emerging environmental problems. If AI tools become more widely adopted in the organizations involved in environmental governance that will further raise questions about who learns. Such questions for future research also have important implications for environmental governance practitioners.

Finally, we encourage our colleagues and students who are primarily interested in the study of learning to consider how they can engage with practitioners and support a learning mindset. Academics can partner with practitioners in an engaged scholarship approach (Van de Ven, 2007) to build novel research questions about learning, provide neutral venues for engaging diverse interests around those questions, and find creative ways to observe, evaluate, and interpret learning. Since our time in the Everglades, we have intentionally partnered with practitioners in, led university-community efforts (Gerlak and Zuniga-Teran, 2020; Gerlak et al., 2022), and served on local and regional advisory boards. Through partnership and service, we believe that researchers can build shared capacity to challenge dominant forms of knowledge in environmental governance. This may require some willingness to produce "activist scholarship" (Tempura et al., 2019) that help shift learning culture in institutions that are stagnating or failing to learn. For our environmental governance processes to fully realize societal goals of equity and justice, we need to step outside our comfort zones and meaningfully engage historically marginalized interests who bring knowledge and information that challenges western assumptions and dominant paradigms.

We are all part of an ecosystem of governance. Supporting the sustainability of that ecosystem – in part through the capacity for learning – is everyone's responsibility. We do not know what the future will hold for our environment, or for our societal and institutional capacity to address environmental issues. What we need are systems that allow us to learn quickly enough to be responsive and resilient in the face of these unknowns. While the emphasis of this closing section is on how to translate lessons from research into practice, researchers obviously need to continue to build new forms of knowledge, through engagement with practitioners, and learn to translate and disseminate knowledge from others. In doing so, we encourage scholars interested in learning to build their own learning communities via workshops, conferences, webinars, and special issues of journals to keep thinking about the learning horizon.

5.5 The Learning Horizon in Environmental Governance

Knowledge of the ways in which environmental governance processes and structures support or impede learning is by no means settled. The evidence we drew upon in this Element needs to be continually tested across more diverse contexts, and updated when our expectations are off base or inaccurate in a particular governance setting. For instance, as we recognized in Section 1, many of the empirical cases of learning in environmental governance are in the Global North. More research in the Global South, and more comparative research – particularly across similar governance issues or types of venues in different political settings – would advance our understanding.

At the same time, existing research may be more representative of collaborative or consensual venues and processes. This can limit our knowledge of processes where barriers to learning are higher. Pushing questions of learning into highly conflictual settings, such as court cases, or highly politicized topics, such as climate governance, can also help us test the boundaries of existing theoretical expectations. Doing so can allow us to probe whether certain contexts simply limit what is learned or who is capable of learning, or whether such learning is dependent on the visibility and impact of evidence or information. For instance, research has explored whether extreme weather events (e.g., flooding, wildfires) result in learning – often via changed beliefs – about climate change mitigation or adaptation measures (e.g., Albright and Crow, 2019; Nikolakis and Roberts, 2022). Ongoing research in this area might help us better understand whether certain types of crises or disasters, or the cumulative effect of multiple disasters, creates learning tipping points for key governance actors, or whether and how other intervening factors such as leadership, governance capacity, or community engagement facilitate learning when such focusing events arise (Birkland, 1997).

Relatedly, the literature tends to focus more on positive instances of learning. We lack robust empirical data on cases where individuals learned, but collective learning was blocked, or actors learned the wrong lesson. Future research can test whether the social and structural features and mechanisms we laid out as drivers of learning can also become learning impediments when they are missing. Or are other mechanisms or factors key to understanding non-learning or blocked learning?

Finally, as governance processes evolve, researchers and practitioners alike need to pay closer attention to when we collectively forget, or unlearn, lessons. Conversely we need to continue to explore what governance features can deepen and enrich our understanding of past lessons in ways that ensure we are not blinded by status quo biases. Our approach to institutionalizing learning in Section 5 aims to foster governance systems that enable such deeper forms of learning. Given the lack of longitudinal assessments of learning in environmental governance, the jury is still out. We hope that our community of learning scholars and interested practitioners takes up the charge we laid out and continues to build upon our current state of learning.

References

Adelle, C., Black, G., & Kroll, F. (2022). Digital storytelling for policy impact: Perspectives from co-producing knowledge for food system governance in South Africa. *Policy Press*, 18, 336–55.

Adler, N. J. (2006). The arts & leadership: Now that we can do anything, what will we do? *Academy of Management Learning and Education*, 5(4), 486–99.

African Activists for Climate Justice Project (AACJ). (nd). *About Us*. https://aacj.africa/#:~:text=About%20Us-,The%20African%20Activists%20for%20Climate%20Justice%20(AACJ)%20project%20%E2%80%93%20a,halthy%20environment%20and%20self%2Ddetermination.

Albright, E. A., & Crow, D. (2019). Beliefs about climate change in the aftermath of extreme flooding. *Climatic Change*, 155(1), 1–17.

Andrade, R., van Riper, C. J., Goodson, D. J., Johnson, D. N., Stewart, W., López-Rodríguez, M. D., Cebrián-Piqueras, M. A., Horcea-Milcu, A. I., Lo, V., & Raymond, C. M. (2023). Values shift in response to social learning through deliberation about protected areas. *Global Environmental Change*, 78, 102630.

Argote, L. (2011). Organizational learning research: Past, present and future. *Management Learning*, 42(4), 439–46.

Argyris, C. and Schön, D. (1996). *Organizational learning II*. Reading, MA: Addison-Wesley.

Argyris, C., & Schön, D. A. (1997). Organizational learning: A theory of action perspective. *Reis*, 77/78, 345–48.

Armitage, D., Marschke, M., & Plummer, R. (2008). Adaptive co-management and the paradox of learning. *Global Environmental Change*, 18(1), 86–98.

Armitage, D., Berkes, F., Dale, A., Kocho-Schellenberg, E., & Patton, E. (2011). Co-management and the co-production of knowledge: Learning to adapt in Canada's Arctic. *Global Environmental Change*, 21(3), 995–1004.

Armitage, D., Dzyundzyak, A., Baird, J., Bodin, Ö., Plummer, R., & Schultz, L. (2018). An approach to assess learning conditions, effects, and outcomes in environmental governance. *Environmental Policy and Governance*, 28(1), 3–14.

Baker, Z., Ekstrom, J. A., Meagher, K. D., Preston, B. L., & Bedsworth, L. (2020). The social structure of climate change research and practitioner engagement: Evidence from California. *Global Environmental Change*, 63, 102074.

Barnett, B. G. (1995). Developing reflection and expertise: Can mentors make the difference? *Journal of Educational Administration*, 33(5), 45–59.

Barrouillet, P. (2015). Theories of cognitive development: From Piaget to today. *Developmental Review*, 38, 1–12.

Bathke, D. J., Haigh, T., Bernadt, T., Wall, N., Hill, H., & Carson, A. (2019). Using serious games to facilitate collaborative water management planning under climate extremes. *Journal of Contemporary Water Research and Education*, 167(1), 50–67.

Baumeister, R. F., Bratslavsky, E., Finkenauer, C., & Vohs, K. D. (2001). Bad is stronger than good. *Review of General Psychology*, 5(4), 323–70.

Beach, D., & Smeets, S. (2022). Once bitten, twice shy: The overgeneralization trap and epistemic learning after policy failure. *Politics and Policy*, 50(6), 1177–202.

Ben-Haim, Y. (2019). Info-Gap decision theory (IG). In V. A. W. J. Marchau, Walker W. E., Bloemen P. J. T. M., & Popper S. W., eds. *Decision making under deep uncertainty: From theory to practice*. Cham: Springer Publishers, pp. 93–116.

Bendt, P., Barthel, S., & Colding, J. (2013). Civic greening and environmental learning in public-access community gardens in Berlin. *Landscape and Urban Planning*, 109(1), 18–30.

Bendtsen, E. B., Clausen, L. P. W., & Hansen, S. F. (2021). A review of the state-of-the-art for stakeholder analysis with regard to environmental management and regulation. *Journal of Environmental Management*, 279, 111773.

Bennett, C., & Howlett, M. (1992). The lessons of learning: Reconciling theories of policy learning and policy change. *Policy Sciences*, 25, 275–94.

Bennett, C. J. (1997). Understanding ripple effects: The cross-national adoption of policy instruments for bureaucratic accountability. *Governance*, 10(3), 213–33.

Benson, L., Petersen, K., & Stein, J. (2007). Anasazi (pre-Columbian Native-American) migrations during the middle-12th and late-13th centuries–were they drought induced? *Climatic Change*, 83(1–2), 187–213.

Berardo, R., & Scholz, J. T. (2010). Self-organizing policy networks: Risk, partner selection, and cooperation in estuaries. *American Journal of Political Science*, 54(3), 632–49.

Betsill, M. M., & Bulkeley, H. (2004). Transnational networks and global environmental governance: The cities for climate protection program. *International Studies Quarterly*, 48(2), 471–93.

Beunen, R., Patterson, J., & van Assche, K. (2017). Governing for resilience: The role of institutional work. *Current Opinion in Environmental Sustainability*, 28, 10–16.

Bietti, L. M., Tilston, O., & Bangerter, A. (2019). Storytelling as adaptive collective sensemaking. *Topics in Cognitive Science*, 11, 710–32.

Birkland, T. A., (1997). *After disaster: Agenda setting, public policy, and focusing events*. Washington, DC: Georgetown University Press.

Bodin, Ö., Crona, B. & Ernstson, H. (2006). Social networks in natural resource management: What is there to learn from a structural perspective? *Ecology and Society*, 11, r2.

Bodin, Ö. (2017). Collaborative environmental governance: Achieving collective action in social-ecological systems. *Science*, 357(6352), 1–8.

Bodin, Ö., Baird, J., Schultz, L., Plummer, R., & Armitage, D. (2020). The impacts of trust, cost and risk on collaboration in environmental governance. *People and Nature*, 2(3), 734–49.

Bomberg, E. (2007). Policy learning in an enlarged European Union: Environmental NGOs and new policy instruments. *Journal of European Public Policy*, 14(2), 248–68.

Bohensky, E. L., & Maru, Y. (2011). Indigenous knowledge, science, and resilience: What have we learned from a decade of international literature on "integration"? *Ecology and Society*, 16(4), 6.

Boris, V. (2017). What makes storytelling so effective for learning? *Harvard Business School Corporate Learning*. www.harvardbusiness.org/what-makes-storytelling-so-effective-for-learning/.

Brewer, M. B. (1999). The psychology of prejudice: Ingroup love and outgroup hate? *Journal of Social Issues*, 55(3), 429–44.

Brulle, R. J., Aronczyk, M., & Carmichael, J. (2020). Corporate promotion and climate change: An analysis of key variables affecting advertising spending by major oil corporations, 1986–2015. *Climatic Change*, 159(1), 87–101.

Brummel, R. F., Nelson, K. C., Souter, S. G., Jakes, P. J., & Williams, D. R. (2010). Social learning in a policy-mandated collaboration: Community wildfire protection planning in the eastern United States. *Journal of Environmental Planning and Management*, 53(6), 681–99.

Burch, S., Gupta, A., Inoue, C. Y. A., Kalfagianni, A., Persson, Å., Gerlak, A. K., Ishii, A., Patterson, J., Pickering, J., Scobie, M., Van der Heijden, J., Vervoort, J., Adler, C., Bloomfield, M., Djalante, R., Dryzek, J., Galaz, V., Gordon, C., Harmon, R., Jinnah, S., & Zondervan, R. (2019). New directions in earth system governance research. *Earth System Governance*, 1, 100006.

Butler, D. M., Volden, C., Dynes, A. M., & Shor, B. (2017). Ideology, learning, and policy diffusion: Experimental evidence. *American Journal of Political Science*, 61(1), 37–49.

Buzinde C. N., Manuel-Navarrete, D., & Swanson, T. (2020) Co-producing sustainable solutions in indigenous communities through scientific tourism. *Journal of Sustainable Tourism*, 28(9),1255–71

Carlile, P. R. (2004). Transferring, translating, and transforming: An integrative framework for managing knowledge across boundaries. *Organizational Science*, 15(5), 555–68.

Chaffin, B. C., Gosnell, H., & Cosens, B. A. (2014). A decade of adaptive governance scholarship: Synthesis and future directions. *Ecology and Society*, 19(3), 56.

Cheng, A. S., Danks, C., & Allred, S. R. (2011). The role of social and policy learning in changing forest governance: An examination of community-based forestry initiatives in the US. *Forest Policy and Economics*, 13(2), 89–96.

Coghlan, A. T., Preskill, H., & Tzavaras-Catsambas, T. (2003). An overview of appreciative inquiry in evaluation. *New Directions for Evaluation*, 100, 5–22.

Crona, B. I., & Parker, J. N. (2012). Learning in support of governance: Theories, methods, and a framework to assess how bridging organizations contribute to adaptive resource governance. *Ecology and Society*, 17(1), 32. https://www.ecologyandsociety.org/vol17/iss1/art32/.

Crossan, M. M., Lane, H., & White, R. E. (1999). An organizational learning framework: From intuition to institution. *Academy of Management Review*, 24(3), 522–37.

Crow, D. A., & Albright, E. A. (2019). Intergovernmental relationships after disaster: State and local government learning during flood recovery in Colorado. *Journal of Environmental Policy and Planning*, 21(3), 257–74.

Crow, D. A., DeLeo, R. A., Albright, E. A., Taylor, K., Birkland, T., Zhang, M., Koebele, E., Jeschke, N., Shanahan, E.A., & Cage, C. (2023). Policy learning and change during crisis: COVID-19 policy responses across six states. *Review of Policy Research*, 40(1), 10–35.

da Silva Wells, C., van Lieshout, R., & Uytewaal, E. (2013). Monitoring for learning and developing capacities in the WASH sector. *Water Policy*, 15(S2), 206–25.

Dale, A., & Armitage, D. (2011). Marine mammal co-management in Canada's Arctic: Knowledge co-production for learning and adaptive capacity. *Marine Policy*, 35(4), 440–49.

Davidson-Hunt, I. J., & O'Flaherty, R. M. (2007). Researchers, indigenous peoples, and place-based learning communities. *Society and Natural Resources*, 20(4), 291–305.

Davis, E. J., Huber-Stearns, H., Cheng, A.S., & Jacobson, M. (2021). Transcending parallel play: Boundary spanning for collective action in wildfire management. *Fire*, 4, 41.

DeCaro, D. A., Arnold, C. A., Boamah, E. F., & Garmestani, A. S. (2017). Understanding and applying principles of social cognition and decision making in adaptive environmental governance. *Ecology and Society*, 22(1), 33.

De Voogt, D. L., & Patterson, J. J. (2019). Exogenous factors in collective policy learning: The case of municipal flood risk governance in the Netherlands. *Journal of Environmental Policy and Planning*, 21(3), 302–19.

Delta Independent Science Board. (2016). *Improving adaptive management in the Sacramento San-Joaquin Delta*. Sacramento, CA: Delta Stewardship Council. https://deltacouncil.ca.gov/pdf/isb/products/2016-02-19-adaptive-management-report.pdf.

Delta Stewardship Council. (2023a). *Delta plan*. Sacramento, CA: Delta Stewardship Council. https://deltacouncil.ca.gov/delta-plan/.

Delta Stewardship Council. (2023b). *Adaptive management*. Sacramento, CA: Delta Stewardship Council. https://deltacouncil.ca.gov/delta-science-program/adaptive-management.

Deverell, E. (2009). Crises as learning triggers: Exploring a conceptual framework of crisis induced learning. *Journal of Contingencies and Crisis Management*, 17(3), 179–88.

Di Giulio, M., & Vecchi, G. (2019). Multilevel policy implementation and the where of learning: The case of the information system for school buildings in Italy. *Policy Sciences*, 52(1), 119–35.

Djalante, R., & Siebenhüner, B. (2021). *Adaptiveness: Changing earth system governance*. Cambridge: Cambridge University Press.

Dow, K., Haywood, B., Kettle, N., & Lackstrom, K. (2013). The role of ad hoc networks in supporting climate change adaptation: A case study from the southeastern United States. *Regional Environmental Change*, 13(1), 1235–44.

Dressel, S., Sjölander-Lindqvist, A., Johansson, M., Ericsson, G., & Sandström, C. (2021). Achieving social and ecological outcomes in collaborative environmental governance: Good examples from Swedish moose management. *Sustainability*, 13(4), 2329.

Dunlop, C. A., & Radaelli, C. M. (2013). Systematising policy learning: From monolith to dimensions. *Political studies*, *61*(3), 599–619.

Dunlop, C. A., & Radaelli, C. M. (2018). The lessons of policy learning: Types, triggers, hindrances and pathologies. *Policy and Politics*, 46(2), 255–72.

Dunning, K. H. (2020). Building resilience to natural hazards through coastal governance: A case study of Hurricane Harvey recovery in Gulf of Mexico communities. *Ecological Economics*, 176, 106759.

Earth System Governance Project. (2018). *Earth System Governance: Science and implementation plan of the Earth System Governance Project*. Utrecht: Earth System Governance Project.

Edmondson, A. C. (2004). Psychological safety, trust, and learning in organizations: A group-level lens. In R. M. Kramer & Cook K. S., eds. *Trust and distrust in organizations: Dilemmas and approaches*. New York: Russell Sage Foundation, pp. 239–72.

Edmondson, A. C (2018). *The fearless organization: Creating psychological safety in the workplace for learning, innovation, and growth*. Hoboken, NJ: Wiley Publishers.

Edmondson, A.C., & Woolley, A. W. (2006). Understanding outcomes of organizational learning interventions. In M. Easterby-Smith & Lyles M. A., eds. *Handbook of organizational learning and knowledge management*. Oxford: Blackwell Publishers, pp. 941–66.

Ernst, A. (2019). Review of factors influencing social learning within participatory environmental governance. *Ecology and Society*, 24(1), 3.

Esguerra, A., & Van der Hel, S. (2021). Participatory designs and epistemic authority in knowledge platforms for sustainability. *Global Environmental Politics*, 21(1), 130–51.

Eshuis, J., & Stuiver, M. (2005). Learning in context through conflict and alignment: Farmers and scientists in search of sustainable agriculture. *Agriculture and Human Values*, 22(2), 137–48.

Fam, D., Mitchell, C., Abeysuriyaa, K., & Meek, T. (2013). Facilitating organizational learning to support decision making and planning for sustainability in the water sector. *Water Policy*, 15, 1094–108.

Fazey, I., Fazey, J. A., & Fazey, D. M. A. (2005). Learning more effectively from experience. *Ecology and Society*, 10(2), 4.

Feldman, D. L., & Ingram, H. M. (2009). Making science useful to decision makers: Climate forecasts, water management, and knowledge networks. *Weather, Climate and Society*, 1, 9–21.

Feldman, M. S., & Rafaeli, A. (2002). Organizational routines as sources of connections and understandings. *Journal of Management Studies*, 39(3), 309–32.

Fierro, R. S. (2016). Enhancing facilitation skills: Dancing with dynamic tensions. *New Directions for Evaluation*, 149, 31–42.

Fischer, A. A (2015). Boundary-Spanning organization for transdisciplinary science on land stewardship: The stewardship network. *Ecology and Society*, 20, 38.

Fitzsimons, D., James, K. T., & Denyer, D. (2011). Alternative approaches for studying shared and distributed leadership. *International Journal of Management Reviews*, 13(3), 313–28.

Folke, C., Hahn, T., Olsson, P., & Norberg, J. (2005). Adaptive governance of social-ecological systems. *Annual Review of Environment and Resource*, 30, 441–73.

Frantzeskaki, N., & Kabisch, N. (2016). Designing a knowledge co-production operating space for urban environmental governance—Lessons from Rotterdam, Netherlands and Berlin, Germany. *Environmental Science and Policy*, 62, 90–8.

Fritz, J. M. (2021). The art of facilitation. In J. M. Fritz, ed. *International clinical sociology*. New York: Springer, pp. 215–36.

Fung, A. (2015). Putting the public back into governance: The challenges of citizen participation and its future. *Public Administration Review*, 75(4), 513–22.

García-Morales, V. J., Jiménez-Barrionuevo, M. M., & Gutiérrez-Gutiérrez, L. (2012). Transformational leadership influence on organizational performance through organizational learning and innovation. *Journal of Business Research*, 65(7), 1040–50.

Garrett, A., MacMullen, P., & Symes, D. (2012). Fisheries as learning systems: Interactive learning as the basis for improved decision making. *Fisheries Research*, 127, 182–87.

Gerlak, A. K., & Heikkila, T. (2011). Building a theory of learning in collaboratives: Evidence from the Everglades Restoration Program. *Journal of Public Administration Research and Theory*, 21(4), 619–44.

Gerlak, A. K., Heikkila, T., Smolinski, S. L., Huitema, D., & Armitage, D. (2018). Learning our way out of environmental policy problems: A review of the scholarship. *Policy Sciences*, 51(3), 335–71.

Gerlak, A. K., Heikkila, T., & Newig, J. (2020). Learning in environmental governance: Opportunities for translating theory to practice. *Journal of Environmental Policy and Planning*, 5, 653–66.

Gerlak, A. K., Jacobs, K. L., McCoy, A. L., Martin, S., Rivera-Torres, M., Murveit, A. M., Leinberger, A. J., & Thomure, T. (2021a). Scenario planning: Embracing the potential for extreme events in the Colorado River Basin. *Climatic Change*, 165(1–2), 27.

Gerlak, A. K., Elder, A., Pavao-Zuckerman, M., Zuniga-Teran, A., & Sanderford, A. R. (2021b). Agency and governance in green infrastructure policy adoption and change. *Journal of Environmental Policy and Planning*, 23(5), 599–615.

Gerlak, A. K., Karambelkar, S., & Ferguson, D. B. (2021c). Knowledge governance and learning: Examining challenges and opportunities in the Colorado River basin. *Environmental Science and Policy*, 125, 219–30.

Gerlak, A. K., Baldwin, B., Zuniga-Teran, A., Colella, T., Elder, A., Bryson, M., Gupta, N., Yang, B., Doyle, T., Heflin, S., & MacAdam, J., . (2022). A collaborative effort to address maintenance of green infrastructure through a university–community partnership. *Socio-Ecological Practice Research*, 4, 1–16.

Gerlak, A. K., & Zuniga-Teran, A. (2020). Addressing injustice in green infrastructure through socio-ecological practice: What is the role of university–community partnerships? *Socio-Ecological Practice Research*, 2(2), 149–59.

Goldstein, B., Wessells, A. T., Lejano, R., & Butler, W. (2015). Narrating resilience: Transforming urban systems through collaborative storytelling. *Urban Studies*, 52(7), 1285–303.

Gronow, A., Brockhaus, M., Di Gregorio, M., Karimo, A., & Ylä-Anttila, T. (2021). Policy learning as complex contagion: How social networks shape organizational beliefs in forest-based climate change mitigation. *Policy Sciences*, 54(3), 529–56.

Gulsrud, N. M., Hertzog, K., & Shears, I. (2018). Innovative forestry governance in Melbourne?: Investigating "green placemaking" as a nature-based solution. *Environmental Research*, 161, 158–67.

Gunderson, L., & Light, S. S., (2006). Adaptive management and adaptive governance in the Everglades ecosystem. *Policy Sciences*, 39, 323–34.

Gupta, J., Termeer, C., Klostermann, J., Meijerink, S., Van den Brink, M., Jong, P., Nooteboom, S., & Bergsma, E. (2010). The adaptive capacity wheel: A method to assess the inherent characteristics of institutions to enable the adaptive capacity of society. *Environmental Science and Policy*, 13(6), 459–71.

Guston, D. H. (2001). Boundary organizations in environmental policy and science: An introduction. *Science, Technology and Human Values*, 26(4), 399–408.

Haas, P. M. (1992). Introduction: Epistemic communities and international policy coordination. *International Organization*, 46, 1–35.

Haas, P. M. (2000). International institutions and social learning in the management of global environmental risks. *Journal of Policy Studies*, 28(3), 558–75.

Haasnoot, M., van 't Klooster, S., & Van Alphen, J. (2018). Designing a monitoring system to detect signals to adapt to uncertain climate change. *Global Environmental Change*, 52, 273–85.

Haug, C., Huitema, D., & Wenzler, I. (2011). Learning through games? Evaluating the learning effect of a policy exercise on European climate policy. *Technological Forecasting and Social Change*, 78(6), 968–81.

Heclo, H. (1974). *Modern social politics in Britain and Sweden: From relief to income maintenance*. New Haven, CT: Yale University Press.

Heikkila, T., & Gerlak, A. K. (2013). Building a conceptual approach to collective learning: Lessons for public policy scholars. *Policy Studies Journal*, 41(3), 484–512.

Heikkila, T., & Gerlak, A. K. (2019). Working on learning: How the institutional rules of environmental governance matter. *Journal of Environmental Planning and Management*, 62(1), 106–23.

Heikkila, T., Gerlak, A. K., & Smith, B. (2023). Diagnosing individual barriers to collective learning: How governance contexts shape cognitive biases. *Journal of European Public Policy*, 1–24, https://doi.org/10.1080/13501763.2023.2251525.

Heikkila, T., Weible, C. M., & Gerlak, A. K. (2020). When does science persuade (or not persuade) in high conflict policy contexts? *Public Administration*, 98(3), 535–50.

Henly-Shepard, S., Gray, S. A., & Cox, L. J. (2015). The use of participatory modeling to promote social learning and facilitate community disaster planning. *Environmental Science and Policy*, 45, 109–22.

Henry, A. D. (2009). The challenge of learning for sustainability: A prolegomenon to theory. *Human Ecology Review*, 16(2), 131–40.

Henry, A. D., & Vollan, B. (2014). Networks and the challenge of sustainable development. *Annual Review of Environment and Resources*, 39, 583–610.

Hill, H., Hadarits, M., Rieger, R., Strickert, G., Davies, E. G. R., & Strobbe, K. M. (2014). The invitational drought tournament: What is it and why is it a useful tool for drought preparedness and adaptation? *Weather and Climate Extremes*, 3, 107–16.

Howlett, M., & Joshi-Koop, S. (2011). Transnational learning, policy analytical capacity, and environmental policy convergence: Survey results from Canada. *Global Environmental Change*, 21(1), 85–92.

Howlett, M., Mukherjee, I., & Koppenjan, J. (2017). Policy learning and policy networks in theory and practice: The role of policy brokers in the Indonesian biodiesel policy network. *Policy and Society*, 36(2), 233–50.

Huitema, D., Cornelisse, C., & Ottow, B. (2010). Is the jury still out? Toward greater insight in policy learning in participatory decision processes – The case of Dutch citizens' juries on water management in the Rhine Basin. *Ecology and Society*, 15(1), 16.

Imperial, M. T., Ospina, S., Johnston, E., O'Leary, R., Thomsen, J., Williams, P., & Johnson, S. (2016). Understanding leadership in a world of shared problems: Advancing network governance in large landscape conservation. *Frontiers in Ecology and the Environment*, 14(3), 126–34.

Innes, J. E., & Booher, D. E. (1999). Consensus building and complex adaptive systems: A framework for evaluating collaborative planning. *Journal of the American Planning Association*, 65(4), 412–23.

Ison, R. L., Collins, K. B., & Wallis, P. J. (2015). Institutionalizing social learning: Towards systemic and adaptive governance. *Environmental Science & Policy*, 53, 105–17.

Interagency Ecological Program (IEP). (2023). *About the Interagency Ecological Program*. Sacramento, CA: State of California. https://iep.ca.gov/About.

Jansen, J. J. P., Vera, D., & Crossan, M. (2009). Strategic leadership for exploration and exploitation: The moderating role of environmental dynamism. *The Leadership Quarterly*, 20(1), 5–18.

Johannessen, Å., Swartling, Å. G., Wamsler, C., Andersson, K., Arran, J. T., Vivas, D. I. H., & Stenström, T. A. (2019). Transforming urban water governance through social (triple-loop) learning. *Environmental Policy and Governance*, 29(2), 144–54.

Johnson, H., & Wilson, G. (2009). *Learning for development*. New York: Zed Books.

Johnson, S. (2006). *The ghost map: The story of London's most terrifying epidemic–and how it changed science, cities, and the modern world*. London: Penguin.

Kahneman, D. (2011). *Thinking, fast and slow*. New York: Farrar, Straus, and Giroux.

Kahneman, D., & Tversky, A. (1979). Prospect theory: An analysis of decision under risk. *Econometrica*, 47, 263–91.

Kamkhaji, J. C., & Radaelli, C. M. (2017). Crisis, learning and policy change in the European Union. *Journal of European Public Policy*, 24(5), 714–34.

Klein, G. (2007). Performing a project premortem. *Harvard Business Review*, 85(9), 18–19.

Kochskämper, E., Koontz, T. M., & Newig, J. (2021). Systematic learning in water governance: Insights from five local adaptive management projects for water quality innovation. *Ecology and Society*, 26(1), 22.

Koebele, E. (2019). Policy learning in collaborative environmental governance processes. *Journal of Environmental Policy and Planning*, 21(3), 242–56.

Koole, B. (2020). Trusting to learn and learning to trust: A framework for analyzing the interactions of trust and learning in arrangements dedicated to instigating social change. *Technological Forecasting and Social Change*, 161, 120260.

Kumnerdpet, W. (2011). Challenging institutional frameworks of governance: Learning from participatory irrigation management in Thailand. In *the 5th International Conference on Globalization: The Scale of Globalization.*

Think Globally, Act Locally, Change Individually in the 21st Century. Ostrava, The Czech Republic, pp. 8–9.

Kunda, Z. (1990). The case for motivated reasoning. *Psychological Bulletin,* 108(3), 480.

Lagadec, P. (1997). Learning processes for crisis management in complex organizations. *Journal of Contingencies and Crisis Management*, 5(1), 24–31.

Leach, W. D., & Sabatier, P.A. (2005). To trust an adversary: Integrating rational and psychological models of collaborative policymaking. *American Political Science Review*, 99(4), 491–503.

Leach, W. D., Weible, C. M., Vince, S. R., Siddiki, S. N., & Calanni, J. C. (2014). Fostering learning through collaboration: Knowledge acquisition and belief change in marine aquaculture partnerships. *Journal of Public Administration Research and Theory*, 24(3), 591–622.

Leck, H., & Roberts, D. (2015). What lies beneath: Understanding the invisible aspects of municipal climate change governance. *Current Opinion in Environmental Sustainability*, 13, 61–67.

Lee, C., & Ma, L. (2020). The role of policy labs in policy experiment and knowledge transfer: A comparison across the UK, Denmark, and Singapore. *Journal of Comparative Policy Analysis: Research and Practice*, 22(4), 281–97.

Lejano, R. P., Haque, E., & Berkes, F. (2021). Co-production of risk knowledge and improvement of risk communication: A three-legged stool. *International Journal of Disaster Risk Reduction*, 64, 102508.

Lejano, R. P., & Ingram, H. (2009). Collaborative networks and new ways of knowing. *Environmental Science and Policy*, 12(6), 653–62.

Levy, J. (1994). Learning and foreign policy. *International Organization*, 48(2), 279–312.

Lindsay, J., Rogers, B. C., Church, E., Gunn, A., Hammer, K., Dean, A. J., & Fielding, K. (2019). The role of community champions in long-term sustainable urban water planning. *Water*, 11(3), 476.

Lipshitz, R., Popper, M., & Friedman, V. J. (2002). A multifacet model of organizational learning. *The Journal of Applied Behavioral Science*, 38(1), 78–98.

Lubell, M., Blomquist, W., & Beutler, L. (2020). Sustainable groundwater management in California: A grand experiment in environmental governance. *Society and Natural Resources*, 33(12), 1447–67.

Mabon, L., Shih, W. Y., Kondo, K., Kanekiyo, H., & Hayabuchi, Y. (2019). What is the role of epistemic communities in shaping local environmental policy? Managing environmental change through planning and greenspace in Fukuoka City, Japan. *Geoforum*, 104, 158–69.

Mackie, D. M., & Smith, E. R. (2017). Group-based emotion in group processes and intergroup relations. *Group Processes & Intergroup Relations*, 20(5), 658–68.

Mahler, J. (1997). Influences of organizational culture on learning in public agencies. *Journal of Public Administration Research and Theory*, 7(4), 519–40.

Mann, M. E. (2021). *The new climate war: The fight to take back our planet*. New York: Public Affairs.

Marchau, V. A. W. J., Walker, W. E., Bloemen, P. J. T. M., & Popper, S. W. (2019). *Decision making under deep uncertainty: From theory to practice*. Cham: Springer Publishers.

Mason, L. (2015). "I disrespectfully agree": The differential effects of partisan sorting on social and issue polarization. *American Journal of Political Science*, 59(1), 128–45.

May, P. J. (1992). Policy learning and failure. *Journal of Public Policy*, 12(4), 331–54.

McConnell, A. (2015). A primer to help navigate the maze. *Public Policy and Administration*, 30(3–4), 221–42.

Meseguer, C. (2005). Policy learning, policy diffusion, and the making of a new order. *The Annals of the American Academy of Political and Social Science*, 598(1), 67–82.

Mezirow, J. (1994). Understanding transformation theory. *Adult Education Quarterly*, 44(4), 222–44.

Michaels, S. (2009). Matching knowledge brokering strategies to environmental policy problems and settings. *Environmental Science and Policy*, 12(7), 994–1011.

Montpetit, É., & Lachapelle, E. (2015). Can policy actors learn from academic scientists?. *Environmental Politics*, *24*(5), 661–80.

Montpetit, É., & Lachapelle, E. (2017). Policy learning, motivated skepticism, and the politics of shale gas development in British Columbia and Quebec. *Policy and Society*, 36(2), 195–214.

Moyson, S., Scholten, P., & Weible, C. M. (2017). Policy learning and policy change: Theorizing their relations from different perspectives. *Policy and Society*, 36(2), 161–77.

Mukhtarov, F., Dieperink, C., Driessen, P., & Riley, J. (2019). Collaborative learning for policy innovations: Sustainable urban drainage systems in Leicester, United Kingdom. *Journal of Environmental Policy and Planning*, 21(3), 288–301.

Munaretto, S., & Huitema, D. (2012). Adaptive co-management in the Venice lagoon? An analysis of current water and environmental management practices and prospects for change. *Ecology and Society*, 17(19). http://dx.doi.org/10.5751/ES-04772-170219.

Muro, M., & Jeffrey, P. (2012). Time to talk? How the structure of dialog processes shapes stakeholder learning in participatory water resources management. *Ecology and Society*, 17(1), 3.

Newell, P., Daley, F., & Twena, M. (2022). *Changing our ways: Behaviour change and the climate crisis. Elements in earth system governance*. Cambridge: Cambridge University Press.

Newig, J., Günther, D. & Pahl-Wostl, C. (2010). Synapses in the network: Learning in governance networks in the context of environmental management. *Ecology and Society*, 15, 24.

Newig J., Kochskamper E., Challies E., & Jager, N. W. (2016). Exploring governance learning: How policymakers draw on evidence, experience and intuition in designing participatory flood risk planning. *Environmental Science and Policy*, 55, 353–60.

Newig, J., Jager, N. W., Kochskämper, E., & Challies, E. (2019). Learning in participatory environmental governance – its antecedents and effects: Findings from a case survey meta-analysis. *Journal of Environmental Policy and Planning*, 21(3), 213–27.

Newman, L. L., & Dale, A. (2005). Network structure, diversity, and proactive resilience building: A response to Tompkins and Adger. *Ecology and Society*, 10(1), r2.

Nickerson, R. S. (1998). Confirmation bias: A ubiquitous phenomenon in many guises. *Review of General Psychology*, 2(2), 175–220.

Nikolakis, W., & Roberts, E. (2022). Wildfire governance in a changing world: Insights for policy learning and policy transfer. *Risk, Hazards & Crisis in Public Policy*, 13(2), 144–64.

Nilsson, M. (2006). The role of assessments and institutions for policy learning: A study on Swedish climate and nuclear policy formation. *Policy Sciences*, 38(4), 225–49.

Nita, A., Fineran, S., & Rozylowicz, L. (2022). Researchers' perspective on the main strengths and weaknesses of Environmental Impact Assessment (EIA) procedures. *Environmental Impact Assessment Review*, 92, 106690.

Norström, A. V., Cvitanovic, C., Löf, M. F., West, S., Wyborn, C., Balvanera, P., Bednarek, A. T., Bennett, E. M., Biggs, R., de Bremond, A., & Campbell, B. M. (2020). Principles for knowledge co-production in sustainability research. *Nature Sustainability*, 3(3), 182–90.

Nye, J. (1987). Nuclear learning and U.S.–Soviet security regimes. *International Organization*, 41(3), 371–402.

O'Mahony, S., & Bechky, B.A. (2008). Boundary organizations: Enabling collaboration among unexpected allies. *Administrative Science Quarterly*, 53, 422–59.

Ohlsson, S. (2011). *Deep learning: How the mind overrides experience*. Cambridge: Cambridge University Press.

Ojha, H., Regmi, U., Shrestha, K. K., Paudel, N. S., Amatya, S. M., Zwi, A. B., Nuberg, I., Cedamon, E., & Banjade, M. R. (2020). Improving science-policy interface: Lessons from the policy lab methodology in Nepal's community forest governance. *Forest Policy and Economics*, 114, 101997.

Ollis, T. A. (2020). Adult learning and circumstantial activism in the coal seam gas protests: Informal and incidental learning in an environmental justice movement. *Studies in the Education of Adults*, 52(2), 215–31.

Olvera-Garcia, J., & Neil, S. (2020). Examining how collaborative governance facilitates the implementation of natural resource planning policies: A water planning policy case from the Great Barrier Reef. *Environmental Policy and Governance*, 30(3), 115–27.

Oreskes, N., & Conway, E. M. (2011). *Merchants of doubt: How a handful of scientists obscured the truth on issues from tobacco smoke to global warming*. New York: Bloomsbury.

Ostrom, E. (2007). Institutional rational choice: An assessment of the institutional analysis and development framework. In P. A. Sabatier, ed. *Theories of the policy process*. Boulder, CO: Westview Press, pp. 21–64.

Ostrom, E. (2009). Building trust to solve commons dilemmas: Taking small steps to test an evolving theory of collective action. In Simon A. Levin, ed. *Games, groups, and the global good, Springer series in game theory*. Berlin: Springer, pp. 207–28.

Özesmi, U., & Özesmi, S. (2003). A participatory approach to ecosystem conservation: Fuzzy cognitive maps and stakeholder group analysis in Uluabat Lake, Turkey. *Environmental Management*, 31(4), 518-31.

Pahl-Wostl, C. (2009). A conceptual framework for analysing adaptive capacity and multi-level learning processes in resource governance regimes. *Global Environmental Change*, 19(3), 354–65.

Pahl-Wostl, C., Becker, G., Knieper, C., & Sendzimir, J. (2013). How multilevel societal learning processes facilitate transformative change: A comparative case study analysis on flood management. *Ecology and Society*, 18(4), 58, https://www.ecologyandsociety.org/vol18/iss4/art58/.

Pahl-Wostl, C., Craps, M., Dewulf, A., Mostert, E., Tabara, D., & Taillieu, T. (2007a). Social learning and water resources management. *Ecology and Society*, 12(2), 5.

Pahl-Wostl, C., Sendzimir, J., Jeffrey, P., Aerts, J., Berkamp, G., & Cross, K. (2007b). Managing change toward adaptive water management through social learning. *Ecology and Society*, 12(2), 30.

Pallett, H., & Chilvers, J. (2013). A decade of learning about publics, participation, and climate change: Institutionalising reflexivity? *Environment and Planning A*, 45, 1162–83.

Palmer, P. J. (2011). *Healing the heart of democracy: The courage to create a politics worthy of the human spirit*. San Francisco, CA: Jossey Bass.

Pattison, A. (2018). Factors shaping policy learning: A study of policy actors in subnational climate and energy issues. *Review of Policy Research*, 35(4), 535–63.

Pescaroli, G., & Alexander, D. (2018). Understanding compound, interconnected, interacting, and cascading risks: A holistic framework. *Risk Analysis*, 38(11), 2245–57.

Plummer, R., Baird, J., Dzyundzyak, A., Armitage, D., Bodin, O., & Schultz, L. (2017). Is adaptive co-management delivering? Examining relationships between collaboration, learning and outcomes in UNESCO biosphere reserves. *Ecological Economics*, 140, 79–88.

Pormon, M. M. M., & Lejano, R. P. (2023). Relational epistemologies for sustainability and resilience towards disasters. *Progress in Disaster Science*, 17, 100272.

Quick, K. S., & Feldman, M. S. (2014). Boundaries as junctures: Collaborative boundary work for building efficient resilience. *Journal of Public Administration Research and Theory*, 24, 673–95.

Radaelli, C. M. (2008). Europeanization, policy learning, and new modes of governance. *Journal of Comparative Policy Analysis*, 10(3), 239–54.

Raymond, C. M., & Cleary, J. (2013). A tool and process that facilitate community capacity building and social learning for natural resource management. *Ecology and Society*, 18(1), 25.

Reed, M. S. (2008). Stakeholder participation for environmental management: A literature review. *Biological Conservation*, 141, 2417–31.

Resh, W., Siddiki, S., & McConnell, W. R. (2014). Does the network centrality of government actors matter? Examining the role of government organizations in aquaculture partnerships. *Review of Policy Research*, 31(6), 584–609.

Resnick, L. B. (2017). Toward a cognitive theory of instruction. In S. G. Paris, Olson, G. M., & Stevenson, H. W., eds. *Learning and motivation in the classroom*. London: Routledge, pp. 5–38.

Ricco, X., & Schultz, C. (2019). Understanding organizational learning during policy implementation: Lessons from U.S. Forest planning. *Journal of Environmental Policy and Planning*, 21(3), 275–87.

Riche, C., Aubin, D., & Moyson, S. (2020). Too much of a good thing? A systematic review about the conditions of learning in governance networks. *European Policy Analysis*, 7(1), 147–64.

Richerson, P. J., & Boyd, R. (2005). *Not by genes alone: How culture transformed human evolution*. Chicago: University of Chicago Press.

Rietig, K. (2019). Leveraging the power of learning to overcome negotiation deadlocks in global climate governance and low carbon transitions. *Journal of Environmental Policy and Planning*, 21(3), 228–41.

Rietig, K. (2021). *Learning in governance: Climate policy integration in the European Union*. Cambridge, MA: The MIT Press.

Rietig, K., & Perkins, R. (2018). Does learning matter for policy outcomes? The case of integrating climate finance into the EU budget. *Journal of European Public Policy*, 25(4), 487–505.

Rijke, J., Brown, R., Zevenbergen, C., Ashley, R., Farrelly, M., Morison, P., & van Herk, S. (2012). Fit-for-purpose governance: A framework to make adaptive governance operational. *Environmental Science and Policy*, 22, 73–84.

Rodela, R. (2011). Social learning and natural resource management: The emergence of three research perspectives. *Ecology and Society*, 16(4), 30.

Rodela, R., Ligtenberg, A., & Bosma, R. (2019). Conceptualizing serious games as a learning-based intervention in the context of natural resources and environmental governance. *Water*, 11(2), 245.

Roome, N., & Wijen, F. (2006). Stakeholder power and organizational learning in corporate environmental management. *Organization Studies*, 27(2), 235–63.

Sabatier, P. A., & Jenkins-Smith, H. (1999). The advocacy coalition framework: An assessment. In P. A. Sabatier, ed. *Theories of the policy process*. Boulder, CO: Westview, pp. 117–66.

Sattler, C., & Schroter, B. (2022). Collective action across boundaries: Collaborative network initiatives as boundary organizations to improve ecosystem services governance. *Ecosystem Services*, 56, 101452.

Schneider, A., & Ingram, H. (1988). Systematically pinching ideas: A comparative approach to policy design. *Journal of Public Policy*, 8, 61–80.

Schneider, A., & Ingram, H. (1990). Behavioral assumptions of policy tools. *The Journal of Politics*, *52*(2), 510–29.

Schusler, T. M., Decker, D. J., & Pfeffer, M. J. (2003). Social learning for collaborative natural resource management. *Society and Natural Resources*, 16(4), 309–26.

Senge, P. (1990). *The fifth discipline: The art and practice of the learning organization*. New York: Currency Doubleday.

Siebenhüner, B. (2008). Learning in international organizations in global environmental governance. *Global Environmental Politics*, 8(4), 92–116.

Siebenhüner, B., Rodela, R., & Ecker, F. (2016). Social learning research in ecological economics: A Survey. *Environmental Science and Policy*, 55, 116–26.

Sims, L., & Sinclair, A. J. (2008). Learning through participatory resource management programs: Case studies from Costa Rica. *Adult Education Quarterly*, 58(2), 151–68.

Sinclair, A. J., Collins, S. A., & Spaling, H. (2011). The role of participant learning in community conservation in the Arabuko-Sokoke Forest, Kenya. *Conservation and Society*, 9(1), 42–53.

Smerek, R. E. (2018). *Organizational learning and performance: The science and practice of building a learning culture*. New York: Oxford University Press.

Sokołowski, M. M., & Heffron, R. J. (2022). Defining and conceptualizing energy policy failure: The when, where, why, and how. *Energy Policy*, 161, 112745.

Stoddart, M. C. J., & Atlin, C. (2022). Hydroelectricity, environmental governance and anti-reflexivity: Lessons from Muskrat Falls. *Water*, 14, 1992.

Stöhr, C., & Chabay, I. (2014). From shouting matches to productive dialogue–establishing stakeholder participation in Polish fisheries governance. *International Journal of Sustainable Development*, 17(4), 403–19.

Strand, M., Rivers, N., Baasch, R., & Snow, B. (2022). Developing arts-based participatory research for more inclusive knowledge co-production in Algoa Bay. *Current Research in Environmental Sustainability*, 4, 100178.

Strickland, A. A., Taber, C. S., & Lodge, M. (2011). Motivated reasoning and public opinion. *Journal of Health Politics, Policy, and Law*, 36(6), 935–44.

Sunstein, C. R. (2006). The availability heuristic, intuitive cost-benefit analysis, and climate change. *Climatic Change*, 77(1), 195–210.

Tajfel, H., & Turner, J. (1979). An integrative theory of intergroup conflict. In W. G. Austin & Worchel, S., eds. *The social psychology of intergroup relations*. Monterey, CA: Brooks/Cole, pp. 33–37.

Tan, J., & Brown, J. (2005). The world café in Singapore: Creating a learning culture through dialogue. *The Journal of Applied Behavioral Science*, 41(1), 83–90.

Tandon, R., Singh, W., Clover, D., & Hall, B. (2016). Knowledge democracy and excellence in engagement. *IDS Bulletin*, 47(6), 19–36.

Tappin, B. M., Leer, L., & McKay, R. T. (2017). The heart trumps the head: Desirability bias in political belief revision. *Journal of Experimental Psychology: General*, 146(8), 1143.

Taylor, K., Jeschke, N., & Zarb, S. (2023). Analyzing the contextual factors that promote and constrain policy learning in local government. *Policy & Politics*, 51(1), 113–30.

Tempura, L., McGarry, D., & Weber, L. (2019). From academic to political rigour: Insights from the "Tarot" of transgressive research. *Ecological Economics*, 164, 106379.

Turnhout, E., Metze, T., Wyborn, C., Klenk, N., & Louder, E. (2020). The politics of co-production: Participation, power, and transformation. *Current Opinion in Environmental Sustainability*, 42, 15–21.

Tversky, A., & Kahneman, D. (1973). Availability: A heuristic for judging frequency and probability. *Cognitive Psychology*, 5(2), 207–32.

Tyng, C. M., Amin, H. U., Saad, M. N., & Malik, A. S. (2017). The influences of emotion on learning and memory. *Frontiers in Psychology*, 8, 1454, https://doi.org/10.3389/fpsyg.2017.01454.

Uhl-Bien, M. E., & Ospina, S. M. (2012). *Advancing relational leadership research: A dialogue among perspectives*. Greenwich, CT: IAP Information Age.

Vagionaki, T. (2018). Blocked learning in Greece: The case of soft-governance. In C. Dunlop, Radaelli, C. & Trein, P., eds. *Learning in public policy—Analysis, modes and outcomes*. London: Palgrave Macmillan, pp. 191–214.

Valin, N., & Huitema, D. (2023). Experts as policy entrepreneurs: How knowledge can lead to radical environmental change. *Environmental Science and Policy*, 142, 21–28.

Van de Kerkhof, M., & Wieczorek, A. (2005). Learning and stakeholder participation in transition processes towards sustainability: Methodological considerations. *Technological Forecasting and Social Change*, 72(6), 733–47.

Van de Ven, A. H. (2007). *Engaged scholarship: A guide for organizational and social research*. Oxford: Oxford University Press.

Veenman, S., & Liefferink, D. (2014). Transnational communication and domestic environmental policy learning. *ESSACHESS-Journal for Communication Studies*, 7(1), 147–67.

Velardi, S., Leahy, J., Collum, K., McGuire, J., & Ladenheim, M. (2021). Adult learning theory principles in knowledge exchange networks among maple syrup producers and beekeepers in Maine. *The Journal of Agricultural Education and Extension*, 27(1), 3–20.

Volden, C., Ting, M. T., & Carpenter, D. P. (2008). A formal model of learning and policy diffusion. *American Political Science Review*, 102(3), 319–32.

Wagner, P. M., & Ylä-Anttila, T. (2020). Can policy forums overcome echo chamber effects by enabling policy learning? Evidence from the Irish climate change policy network. *Journal of Public Policy*, 40(2), 194–211.

Walters, C. J., & Holling, C. S. (1990). Large-scale management experiments and learning by doing. *Ecology*, 70, 2060–68.

Ward, S., Forrow, D., Kirk, S., Worthington, R., Paling, N., Stacey, F., & Brunt, O. (2024). Visualising, illustrating and communicating future water visions to support learning and sustainability transitions. *Water*, 16(14), 1–23.

Weible, C. M., Olofsson, K. L., & Heikkila, T. (2023). Advocacy coalitions, beliefs, and learning: An analysis of stability, change, and reinforcement. *Policy Studies Journal*, 51(1), 209–29.

Weible, C. M., Pattison, A., & Sabatier, P. A. (2010). Harnessing expert-based information for learning and the sustainable management of complex socio-ecological systems. *Environmental Science and Policy*, 13(6), 522–34.

Witteveen, L., van Arensbergen, P., & Fliervoet, J. M. (2022). Design and development of mediated participation for environmental governance transformation: Experiences with community art and visual problem appraisal. *Central European Journal of Communication*, 15 (30), 112–31.

Wolfram, M. (2019). Learning urban energy governance for system innovation: An assessment of transformative capacity development in three South Korean cities. *Journal of Environmental Policy and Planning*, 21(1), 30–45.

Woodhill, B. (2019). M&E as learning: Rethinking the dominant paradigm. In B. de Graaff, ed. *Monitoring and evaluation of soil conservation and watershed development projects*. Boca Raton, FL: CRC Press, pp. 83–110.

Wyborn, C. (2015). Connectivity conservation: Boundary objects, science narratives and the co-production of science and practice. *Environmental Science and Policy*, 51, 292–303.

Yanguas, P. (2021). *What have we learned about learning? Unpacking the relationship between knowledge and organizational change in development agencies*. Bonn: German Development Institute.

Young, O. R. (2023). *Addressing the grand challenges of planetary governance: The future of the global political order. Elements in Earth System Governance*. Cambridge: Cambridge University Press.

Yu, D. J., Shin, H. C., Perez, I., Anderies, J. M., & Janssen, M. A. (2016). Learning for resilience-based management: Generating hypotheses from a behavioral study. *Global Environmental Change*, 37, 69–78.

Zhang, F., & Zhu, L. (2019). Enhancing corporate sustainable development: Stakeholder pressures, organizational learning, and green innovation. *Business Strategy and the Environment*, 28(6), 1012–26.

Zurba, M., Petriello, M. A., Madge, C., McCarney, P., Bishop, B., McBeth, S., Denniston, M., Bodwitch, H. & Bailey, M. (2022). Learning from knowledge co-production research and practice in the twenty-first century: Global lessons and what they mean for collaborative research in Nunatsiavut. *Sustainability Science*, 17(2), 449–67.

Acknowledgments

In writing this Element, we are particularly grateful to Julia Davies for her extraordinary research support and Amy Jorgensen for her superb design skills. We also deeply appreciate the richness of engagement with our colleagues and students in our respective universities and research centers, which has sharpened our thinking and pushed us in new directions. Finally, we cannot thank our families enough for their endless support and inspiration, and for giving us the time and space to build a long-lasting academic and personal friendship. It is through many years of friendship that our ideas on learning have flourished.

About the Authors

Tanya Heikkila is a Professor in the School of Public Affairs at the University of Colorado Denver, where she co-directs the Center for Policy and Democracy. Her research focuses on how policy can be designed to facilitate collaboration and resolve conflicts. She directs her school's MPP program and MPA concentration in environmental policy.

Andrea K. Gerlak is a Professor in the School of Geography, Development and Environment and Director of the Udall Center for Studies in Public Policy at the University of Arizona. She studies collaboration, community engagement, and equity. She was a co-author on the latest ESG Science Plan and is a Senior Research Fellow with the ESG.

Cambridge Elements

Earth System Governance

About the Series

Linked with the Earth System Governance Project, this exciting new series will provide concise but authoritative studies of the governance of complex socio-ecological systems, written by world-leading scholars. Highly interdisciplinary in scope, the series will address governance processes and institutions at all levels of decision-making, from local to global, within a planetary perspective that seeks to align current institutions and governance systems with the fundamental 21st Century challenges of global environmental change and earth system transformations.

Elements in this series will present cutting edge scientific research, while also seeking to contribute innovative transformative ideas towards better governance. A key aim of the series is to present policy-relevant research that is of interest to both academics and policy-makers working on earth system governance.

More information about the Earth System Governance project can be found at: www .earthsystemgovernance.org.

Cambridge Elements ☰

Earth System Governance

Elements in the Series

Changing Our Ways: Behaviour Change and the Climate Crisis
Peter Newell, Freddie Daley and Michelle Twena

The Carbon Market Challenge: Preventing Abuse Through Effective Governance
Regina Betz, Axel Michaelowa, Paula Castro, Raphaela Kotsch, Michael Mehling, Katharina Michaelowa and Andrea Baranzini

Addressing the Grand Challenges of Planetary Governance: The Future of the Global Political Order
Oran R. Young

Adaptive Governance to Manage Human Mobility and Natural Resource Stress
Saleem H. Ali, Martin Clifford, Dominic Kniveton, Caroline Zickgraf and Sonja Ayeb-Karlsson

The Emergence of Geoengineering: How Knowledge Networks Form Governance Objects
Ina Möller

The Normative Foundations of International Climate Adaptation Finance
Romain Weikmans

Just Transitions: Promise and Contestation
Dimitris Stevis

A Green and Just Recovery from COVID-19?
Kyla Tienhaara, Tom Moerenhout, Vanessa Corkal, Joachim Roth, Hannah Ascough, Jessica Herrera Betancur, Samantha Hussman, Jessica Oliver, Kabir Shahani and Tianna Tischbein

The Politics of Deep Time
Frederic Hanusch

Trade and the Environment: Drivers and Effects of Environmental Provisions in Trade Agreements
Clara Brandi, Jean-Frédéric Morin

Building Capabilities for Earth System Governance
Jochen Prantl, Ana Flávia Barros-Platiau, Cristina Yumie Aoki Inoue, Joana Castro Pereira, Thais Lemos Ribeiro and Eduardo Viola

Learning for Environmental Governance: Insights for a More Adaptive Future
Tanya Heikkila and Andrea K. Gerlak

A full series listing is available at www.cambridge.org/EESG

For EU product safety concerns, contact us at Calle de José Abascal, 56–1°, 28003 Madrid, Spain or eugpsr@cambridge.org.

www.ingramcontent.com/pod-product-compliance
Ingram Content Group UK Ltd.
Pitfield, Milton Keynes, MK11 3LW, UK
UKHW022146080726
473066UK00010B/794

* 9 7 8 1 0 0 9 4 6 1 1 2 2 *